C H I

GOOD STORIES REVEAL as much, or more, about a locale as any map or guidebook. Whereabouts Press is dedicated to publishing books that will enlighten a traveler to the soul of a place. By bringing a country's stories to the English-speaking reader, we hope to convey its culture through literature. Books from Whereabouts Press are essential companions for the curious traveler, and for the person who appreciates how fine writing enhances one's experiences in the world.

"Coming newly into Spanish, I lacked two essentials—a childhood in the language, which I could never acquire, and a sense of its literature, which I could."

—Alastair Reid, *Whereabouts:*
Notes on Being a Foreigner

CHINA

A TRAVELER'S LITERARY COMPANION

EDITED BY

KIRK A. DENTON

WHEREABOUTS PRESS
BERKELEY, CALIFORNIA

Published by
Whereabouts Press
Berkeley, California
www.whereaboutspress.com

Distributed to the trade by PGW / Perseus Distribution.

Library of Congress Cataloging-in-Publication Data

China : a traveler's literary companion /
edited by Kirk A. Denton.
p.   cm. — (Traveler's literary companions ; 15)
ISBN-13: 978-1-883513-23-8 (alk. paper)
ISBN-10: 1-883513-23-5 (alk. paper)
1. Chinese fiction—20th century—Translations into English.
2. China—Fiction.
I. Denton, Kirk A., 1955–
PL2658.E8C45   2008
895.1'30108—dc22
2008020187

5 4 3 2 1

Contents

To Virginia Denton
on the occasion of her eightieth birthday

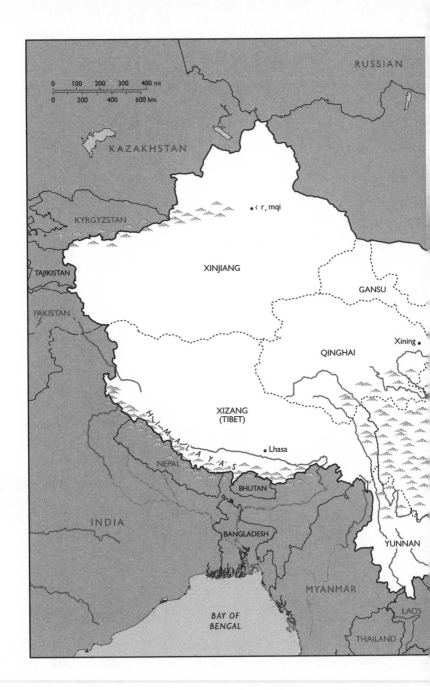

Preface

Chinese writers of the modern era—who have until very recently come mostly from rural areas or small towns in the interior—have had a difficult and problematic relationship with their native places. On the one hand, as with the prototypical departure of Juehui from his feudal home at the end of Ba Jin's novel *Family* (1931), they exalt in leaving their rural homes, families, and the tradition they represent to embrace the metropolis and its modern values.

> A new emotion gradually possessed Juehui. He didn't know whether it was joy or sorrow, but one thing was clear—he was leaving his family. Before him was an endless stretch of water sweeping steadily forward, bearing him to an unfamiliar city. There, all that was new was developing—new activities, new people, new friends. This river, this blessed river, was taking him away from the home he had lived in for eighteen years to a city and people he had never seen. The prospect dazzled him; he had not time to regret the life he had cast behind. For the last time, he looked back. "Goodbye," Juehui said softly. He turned to watch the on-rushing river, the green water that never for an instant halted its rapidly advancing flow. (from Ba Jin's *Family*)

On the other hand, like the bees and the flies in Lu Xun's story "Upstairs in a Wineshop" (1924), these writers always return:

> "When I was a kid, I used to think that bees and flies were absurd and pathetic. I'd watch the way they'd light someplace, get spooked by something, and then fly away. After making a small circle, they'd always come back again and land just exactly where they had been before. Who could have imagined that someday, having made my own small circle, I would fly back too? And who would ever have expected that you would do the same thing? Couldn't you have managed to fly a little farther away?" (spoken by Lu Weifu in Lu Xun's "Upstairs in the Wineshop")

Since the early twentieth century, Chinese writers and intellectuals have been at once attracted to and repelled by both the modern metropolis and the rural home. Movement back and forth between the two spaces (and what they represent culturally) has been one of the defining features of modern Chinese literature.

The earliest of the stories included in this volume, Lu Xun's "Hometown" (1921) establishes the paradigmatic struggle modern intellectuals faced between the universal values of the metropolis and the particularity of home. A modern intellectual trained in Western knowledge, the first-person narrator of the story returns home after a twenty-year absence. He finds a drab place that does not mesh with his nostalgic memories. At the same time, when he recalls his marvelous experiences with his childhood friend Runtu, it is as though he momentarily seems to recapture the beauty of his lost homeland.

From the early twentieth century Chinese writers,

especially those of the May Fourth generation in the late 1910s and 1920s, embraced modernity in a heroic and unwavering attack on tradition in the name of the nation—China. But the China they imagined was quite different from the one they saw in reality, with its weak central government, powerful local warlords, and foreign-controlled concessions in its major coastal cities. To this day, how to define "China" is not self-evident. For some, it refers to the People's Republic of China, a socialist nation founded in 1949 and currently experiencing convulsive economic and social changes. For others, China is more of a cultural construct that also comprises Taiwan, Hong Kong, and diasporic Chinese-speaking communities. Whether we take the narrow political view or the broader cultural view, China is a vast and culturally complex space that is made up of scores of different ethnic groups and, within the dominant Han ethnicity, a dizzying array of local dialects and subcultures.

Even as they struggled within this cultural diversity to imagine themselves as belonging to a unified political or cultural community and to use literature to respond to universal concerns, Chinese writers have been drawn to the particularity of their homes, to the familiar land-scapes of their youths, to local dialects and regional customs. This volume presents Chinese short fiction and a few excerpts from longer works that evoke a strong sense of place, a place that can be real or imagined but that is usually closely associated with their authors' actual homes. Since China was, at least until very recently, primarily an agricultural society, the places described in many of these stories are rural. The reader will travel to the idyllic mountains and streams of West Hunan (Shen Congwen's "Meijin, Baozi, and the White Kid"); a picturesque water town and the silkworm-raising country of Zhejiang (Lu Xun's "Hometown" and Mao Dun's "Spring Silkworms," respectively); the high plateau of western Sichuan where Tibetan culture intermingles with that of Han Chinese (Alai's "Fish"); the primitive vitality of the sorghum fields of Gaomi county in Shandong (Mo Yan's "Old Gun"); the poverty of village life in Henan (Yan Lianke's "White Bristle, Black Bristles"); and the pastoral yet violent world of the northeast province of Heilongjiang (Xiao Hong's "On the Oxart").

As any traveler to China soon discovers, however, China is not just mountains and rice paddies; it has protean metropolises that are growing at a truly frightening pace. Not surprisingly, several of the writers included here—some of them "natives," others transplants—set their stories in such cities as Beijing (Wang Shuo's "Hot and Cold, Measure for Measure"), Shanghai (Zhang Ailing's "Sealed Off"; Wang Anyi's "The Longtang"), Hong Kong (Xi Xi's "The Floating City"), and Taipei (Chu T'ien-hsin's "Man of La Mancha").

Written from 1921 to 2003, the stories encompass the history of modern Chinese literature and cover a gamut of styles, from the realism of Mao Dun, to the modernism of Zhang Ailing, to the postmodern sensibility of Xi Xi and Chu T'ien-hsin. Whether with rural or urban settings, these are modern stories responding to very modern concerns: the place of tradition in modernity; changing morality and social values in the new market economy; the problem of the self in a society that emphasizes collective desires; the search for a missing past in a present that seems empty and meaningless; the effects of globalization; poverty and social disenfranchisement; the nature of political power; and cultural identity in a postmodern world. Some authors exhibit a difficult and problematic relationship with the places they depict, whereas others embrace those places in more sympathetic and nostalgic ways. Both types of representations grow out of the trauma of modernity itself. Given the disruptions and displacements of twentieth-century Chinese social and political life, it is little wonder that place becomes a key marker in its works of literature.

Kirk A. Denton
April 2008

文学

Hometown

Lu Xun

BRAVING THE BONE-COLD WEATHER, I was headed back to my hometown, a hometown from which I was separated by over six hundred miles and more than twenty years.

It was in the depth of winter and as I drew closer to the place where I'd grown up, the sky clouded over and a cold wind whistled into the cabin of my boat. Through a crack in the canopy, I peered out into the distance. Scattered across the distant horizon, towns and villages came into view under the vast and graying sky: they were drab,

---

LU XUN (1881–1936), sometimes called the father of modern Chinese literature, wrote short fiction, prose poems, and essays. His fiction and early essays are generally seen as part of the larger May Fourth New Culture movement (1915–25), which attacked the Confucian tradition as stultifying to individual and national development. His "Diary of a Madman" and "The True Story of Ah Q" are allegories that present Chinese society as cannibalistic and its tradition as mind-numbing. In a less polemical mode, "Hometown" (1921) expresses the problematic relationship Chinese intellectuals of the day had with their hometowns, at once barren and impoverished and the source of wondrous memories of sparkling seas, watermelon patches, and the mysterious *zha*.

---

desolate, devoid of any semblance of life. I was assailed
by a depression against which I was utterly powerless.
No! This was not the countryside I had recalled time and
again for more than twenty years. The area I remembered
was far, far more lovely. And yet, had you demanded that
I summon its beauties from the recesses of memory or
catalog its various excellences, no concrete image would
have appeared in my mind's eye and I would have been
unable to reply. My "hometown" was probably nothing
more than what lay before me. "This is probably what
it really was like," I told myself. "To be sure, there are
no signs of progress, but then again it's probably not so
depressing as I seem to feel at the moment either. Perhaps
it's just that my attitude has changed, especially since I'm
not coming back in a happy mood to begin with."

My sole purpose in coming back this time was to bid my
home an everlasting farewell. The old family compound
in which members of our clan had lived for so many years
had already been sold lock, stock, and barrel to people of
another surname. The transaction was to be completed
by the end of the year. In the short interim before the
New Year, we would have to take our final leave of those
comfortable old rooms and move away from this familiar
countryside to the strange and faraway place where I now
earned my keep.

Early the next morning I stood before the gate of our
family compound. Up on the tile roof, broken stalks of
withered vines trembled in the wind and made plain the
reason it had not been possible to keep those old rooms
from changing hands. The pervading silence suggested
that several branches of the family must have already

moved out. By the time I made my way back to the rooms that our branch occupied, my mother had already come out to greet me. My eight-year-old nephew Hong'er darted out from behind her.

Though she was obviously happy to see me, I also read hints of melancholy in her face. She bade me sit down and rest, gave me some tea, but avoided any mention of the impending move. Hong'er, whom I had never seen before, stood off at a distance observing me.

At long last we broached the subject of moving. I said I had already rented a place for us and had even bought a few sticks of furniture. I explained that we would have to sell our household goods down here and then use that money to buy whatever else we might need up north. Mother readily assented. She already had our baggage pretty much gathered together and ready to go. On her own initiative, she had even sold the heavy furniture that couldn't readily be moved. She had not yet, however, been able to collect the money people owed her for it.

"As soon as you've rested a day or so, you can make the rounds of our relatives and then we'll be all set," she told me.

"Yes, Mother."

"And don't forget to see Runtu. He asks for you every time he comes by. Says he would really like to see you again. I told him around what day you'd be back, so he *could* show up most anytime."

Instantaneously, a marvelous scene flashed before my eyes: a round moon hanging against a blue-black sky, beneath it a stretch of sandy ground planted with emerald-green watermelons stretching as far as the eye could see, and standing in the midst of all those melons a twelve-year-old boy, a silver ring around his neck, a pitchfork in his hand. Suddenly and with all his might the boy stabs at a *zha* [badger], but the crafty animal makes a lightning turn, runs back between his legs, and makes good its escape.

The boy in that scene was Runtu. Back when I first met him—it will soon be thirty years ago—I couldn't have been much more than ten myself. Since my father was still alive at the time, our family was still fairly well-to-do, and I was something of a "young gentleman." That particular year it was incumbent upon our branch of the clan to perform a certain sacrifice that rolled around, or so it was said, only once every thirty-odd years. Consequently it was to be an occasion of great solemnity.

During the first month, images of our ancestors would be displayed on the altar. The offerings set out before them would be lavish and the sacrificial utensils exquisite. With so many people participating, it would be necessary to guard against theft. However, we had only one "busy-monther" to help out and he already had more work than he could keep up with. And so he suggested that his son Runtu be brought in to keep an eye on the sacrificial vessels. (Down home, workers were divided into three categories: if they worked the whole year long for one family, they were "yearlongs"; if they worked by the day, they were "short-timers"; and if they tilled their own land but worked for a specific family just during the holidays or when rents were being collected, they were "busy-monthers.")

Since I had heard about Runtu for a long time, I was glad when father agreed. I knew he was about my own age. He'd been born in the *run* [leap] month and among the five elements he was lacking only in *tu* [earth], so his father had called him Runtu. Best of all, Runtu knew all about how to set snares and catch birds!

From that time on I looked forward eagerly to the New Year, for I knew that when it came so would Runtu. It seemed that *this* year would never end. But the day did finally arrive when Mother summoned me to announce that Runtu had come and was now in the kitchen. I ran as fast as my legs would carry me.

He had a purplish round face and wore a little felt hat. You could tell that his father loved him very much, because around his neck he wore a large, shimmering silver ring. That meant that his father had feared he might die during childhood and had taken him before a statue of the Buddha where, in exchange for the protection of his son, he had promised to do something for the Buddha in return. It was then that they would have put that neckring on to show that Runtu was tied to life and protected by Buddha.

Runtu was shy with the adults around our house but wasn't at all timid with me, and would talk a blue streak whenever we were by ourselves. Before half the day was out, we had actually gotten to know each other quite well. I can't recall what we talked about—I only remember how excited and happy Runtu was. He told me that this was the first time he'd ever been to town and that he had already seen all sorts of strange and wondrous things he'd never even dreamed of before.

The next day I wanted him to catch birds. "Can't right now. You have to have lots of snow. Out by the ocean where we live, I always wait till there's a good snowfall. Then I sweep a place nice and clean, take a little stick, and prop up a big, big bamboo basket. I sprinkle some grain underneath and tie a string to the bottom of the stick. Then I back way, way off and wait for the birds to come. One little tug and I've got them. A little bit of everything—bluebacks, hornchicks, paddychicks, pigeons . . ."

How I longed for snow!

"It's kind of cold now, but you oughta come out our way in the summer. Days, we could go out to the beach and collect shells—reds, blues, ghost-scarer, Guanyin hands. Nights, when Dad and me go to guard the watermelon patch, you could go right along with us."

"Are you afraid people are going to steal your melons?"

"Nope. If somebody happens to be walkin' by and picks one 'cause he's thirsty, we don't take that as stealin'. What we're lookin' out for are badgers, porcupines, and *zha*. When the moon's out and you hear a *crunch crunch*, you know you've got a *zha* bitin' into a melon. You grab your pitchfork and . . ."

At the time I didn't know what sort of thing a *zha* was to begin with—still don't as a matter of fact—but somehow or other I felt it must look like some sort of little dog and be fierce as all get-out.

"Won't it bite you?"

"Well, you've got your pitchfork, right? You sneak up on him and when you've got him in sight, you let him have it. Are those little guys ever quick on their feet! They'll turn around and run right back between your legs if you don't watch 'em. They've got these coats all slippery-slick, like oil, and . . ."

I had never dreamed that the world was so full of so many new and marvelous things. Just to think that the seashore had all those wonderful colored shells to offer! And even watermelons had a danger-filled story behind them that I'd never suspected. All I'd known was that you buy them in fruit stores.

"Out there by the seashore just before the spring tides, you'll see a whole bunch of jumperfish hoppin' around all over the place. They've got these two little legs on 'em just like frogs and . . ."

Wow! Runtu's mind was an inexhaustible treasure-house of exotic things, things my everyday friends knew nothing about, for while Runtu was out there by the sea, they—like me—had nothing to look out on but the square patch of sky that was visible above the high walls of a family courtyard.

Unfortunately the first month of the New Year came to an end and Runtu had to go home. I wailed. He cried too. Then he hid in our kitchen and refused to come out. In the end, however, his father took him away. Later on he sent me a package of shells by way of his father, and some beautiful bird feathers too. And I also sent him some things a few times after that, but I never saw him again.

Now, when my mother said that Runtu might drop by, memories of my boyhood suddenly came alive again as though illumined by a brilliant flash of lightning. For a fraction of a second, I even seemed to recapture that beautiful homeland I thought I had lost.

"Great!" I said. "How . . . how's he doing these days?"

"Now? Well, things aren't going at all well for him." Mother turned and looked outside as she answered. "*Those* people are back again. Pretend they're looking at the furniture and then make off with whatever they can get hold of. I'd better go out and keep an eye on them."

Mother got up and went out. I could hear the voices of several women outside the door. I motioned to Hong'er to come over and chat with me. I asked him if he knew how to write yet and if he was looking forward to our trip.

"Will we get to ride a train?"

"Yes."

"A boat, too?"

"First we take the boat and then . . ."

"Would you look at him now! He's even got a beard!" A strange, shrill voice suddenly sliced through the air.

Startled, I quickly raised my head and saw a woman of fifty or so standing before me. Her cheekbones protruded and her lips were thin. Wearing a pair of trousers (she hadn't tied a skirt over them), hands on her hips, legs wide apart, she stood balanced on a pitiful little pair of bound feet, looking for all the world like a pair of compasses out of someone's drafting kit.

"Don't recognize me, huh? I used to hold you in my arms when you were just a kid!"

I was even more at a loss. Fortunately my mother came back in at this juncture and said, "He's been away a good many years and he's forgotten everything." Then she turned to me. "But you really ought to remember her. She's Second Sister Yang. You know, the woman who lived kitty-corner to our place and ran the beancurd shop."

Now I remembered. When I was a child there had been a Second Sister Yang sitting from one end of the day to the other in the beancurd shop diagonally across from us. People called her the "Beancurd Beauty."

Back then she used to powder her face, and her cheekbones weren't so high, nor were her lips so thin. What was more, since she had always been seated, I had never before seen this "compasses" pose of hers. Back then people used to say that she was the reason the shop did such a surprisingly good business. No doubt because of my tender age, I must have been immune to the alchemy of her charms, for I had forgotten her completely. Thus, "Compasses" was more than a little put out with me. She looked at me with utter disdain and the kind of smile that one might wear upon discovering a Frenchman who had never heard of Napoleon or an American who didn't know who Washington was.

Her laugh was cold. "Forgot, huh? Case of the higher you go, the snootier you—"

"How could I ever be like that . . . why I . . ." Completely flustered, I stood up.

"Well in that case, Elder Brother Xun, I'll put it right up front. You're rich now and it's not all that easy to move big, heavy stuff anyway, so why not let me take all this rickety old furniture off your hands. Poor folks like us can still get a lotta use out of it."

"I'm not rich at all. I have to sell this furniture just to—"

"Come off it. I know you're a big official—a *Daotai*, they say. And you're gonna stand there and tell me you're not rich? You've got three concubines and an eight-man sedan chair team to carry you around wherever you wanna go. Not rich? Hah! You can't put anything over on me!"

I knew it would make no difference no matter what I said, so I held my peace and simply stood there.

"Yup, it's true all right. The more money they get, the less they'll turn loose. And the less they turn loose, the more they get!" Compasses angrily turned her back to me and slowly walked away, issuing a steady stream of chatter as she went. On her way out, she picked up a pair of my mother's gloves and shoved them into the waistband of her trousers.

During the next few days clansmen and relatives who lived nearby came around to pay visits. I met these social obligations as best I could, stealing time from them whenever possible to finish packing.

One very cold afternoon just after lunch I was sitting and drinking tea when I heard someone come in from the outside. When I turned around to look I couldn't help but start with surprise. I scrambled to my feet and rushed over to welcome him.

It was Runtu. Although I recognized him right off, he was not at all the Runtu who lived in my memory. He seemed twice as tall now. The round and ruddy face of yesteryear had already turned pale and gray, and it was etched with deep wrinkles. The rims of his eyes were swollen and red just like his father's. I knew that most farmers who worked close to the sea got that way because of the wind. He was wearing a battered old felt hat, and his cotton clothes were so thin that he was shivering. His hand held a paper package along with his pipe. They were not the smooth and nimble hands that I remembered. Now they were rough, clumsy, and as cracked as pine bark.

I was beside myself with enthusiasm, but didn't know how to begin and simply said, "Brother Runtu, you've come . . ."

There was so much I wanted to say. There were so many words waiting to gush out one after the other like pearls on a string: hornchicks, jumperfish, Guanyin hands, *zha*— but at the same time I was aware of something damming them up inside me, so that they simply swirled around in my brain without a single one coming out.

As he stood there his expression was a mixture of happiness and melancholy. His lips began to move, but not a single word came out. Finally he assumed a very respectful attitude and addressed me in a loud clear voice: "Master!"

I shuddered as I realized what a wretched, thick wall now stood between us. I too was at a loss for words. He turned around and said, "Shuisheng, kowtow to the Master." He grabbed a child who up to this point had been hiding behind him and hauled him around front. This boy was Runtu—twenty years ago, although somewhat paler and thinner than his father had been. The only real difference was that Shuisheng had no silver neckring. "This is my fifth. Hasn't been out and around much, so he's pretty shy."

Mother and Hong'er must have heard us talking because they came down from upstairs.

"Old Missus. I got your letter a long time back. You don't know how happy I was to hear the Master was comin' home," said Runtu.

"Hey, what in the world's come over you that you're so formal. You two used to call each other 'Brother.' Just call him 'Brother Xun' the way you used to."

"Ah, the Old Missus is really too . . . What kind of manners would that be? We were just kids then. We didn't know any better." While Runtu was talking, he was also trying to get Shuisheng to bow to my mother, but the boy was very embarrassed and stuck like glue to his father's back.

"Is that Shuisheng, your fifth?" Mother asked. "To him we're all strangers. No wonder he's so shy. Why not let him and Hong'er go out together and play."

When Hong'er heard that, he immediately ran over and greeted the boy. Shuisheng wasn't the least bit shy with, him, and apparently feeling very much at ease, went outside with my nephew to play. Mother asked Runtu to have a seat. He hesitated for a bit but finally sat down and leaned his long pipe against the table. He handed the paper package across to me and said, "We don't have much of anything in the winter, but these dried peas are ones I sunned myself. Please accept them, Master . . ."

I asked how he was doing. He shook his head.

"Things are pretty rough. Even my sixth is old enough to help out now, but still with all the fightin' and people wantin' money of you every place you turn—you can never be sure how much—and what with all the bad harvests, we just never seem to have enough to eat. When you *do* take whatever crop you've got and head off to market, you've gotta pay a whole bunch of taxes before you ever get there. Ends up so you don't even get back what you've put into it. But if you *don't* take it to market, it's just gonna rot in the field anyway . . .

He stopped talking but continued to shake his head. There was no movement in any of the wrinkles that life had etched upon him and one would have thought that his face was carved from stone. He probably felt all the pain, but could not find the words to express it. He sat in silence for a while and then picked up his pipe and began to smoke.

Through further questioning, Mother learned that he still had much to do at home and would have to leave tomorrow. She also found out that he'd gone without lunch and told him to go into the kitchen and make himself a little something.

After he went out, Mother and I both sighed at his plight: too many children, famine, harsh taxes, soldiers, bandits, officials, gentryfolk—everything had plagued until he'd become the lifeless wooden figure we saw today. Mother said that we ought to see to it that he got as much of what we weren't going to take with us as possible. So we told him to take whatever he wanted.

He selected a few things that very afternoon—two long tables, an incense burner, some candlesticks, and a set of scales. He also asked for the ashes from our kitchen stove. (We cooked with rice stalks, and the ashes would provide good fertilizer for the sandy soil out his way.) He gathered everything together and said he would come for it in a boat the day we moved out.

We chatted a bit more that night, but none of it amounted to anything. Early the next morning he took Shuisheng and headed back on home.

Nine days later the time for our departure finally arrived. Runtu came early in the morning. Shuisheng wasn't with him this time, but he'd brought along a five-year-old girl to keep an eye on the boat. We were so busy that we had no time to chat. Several other people came by, some to see us off, others to get things, and still others to get things *and* to see us off. By the time we boarded the boat that afternoon, the old house had been swept clean of old and used things of every imaginable size and description.

As we proceeded upriver, the twilight-green mountains on either bank took on deeper hues and joined together in a single blue-green mass as they fled away into the distance behind the stern. Hong'er and I leaned against the window and watched the dimming landscape. Suddenly he asked, "Uncle, when are we coming back?"

"Coming back? What are you doing thinking about coming back before we've even left?"

"But Shuisheng invited me to go have some fun at his place." Engrossed by thoughts of his new friend, Hong'er opened his large black eyes even wider in fascination.

Mother and I weren't immune to nostalgia ourselves, and began talking about Runtu again. She told me that ever since she'd started packing, Second Sister Yang—the Beancurd Beauty—had never let a single day pass without coming by. Just the day before yesterday she had retrieved a dozen or so plates from the pile of rice-stalk ashes. After questioning my mother, Second Sister Yang concluded that they must have been hidden there by Runtu so that he could make off with them when he came for the other stuff. Having made this discovery, she apparently felt that she'd rendered us a rewardable service, for she picked up the dog-crazer without so much as a by-your-leave and took off with it just as fast as her legs would carry her. (The dog-crazer was a device we used back home in raising chickens. It consisted of a wooden bowl covered with a lattice-like arrangement wide enough for the chickens to poke their heads through, but too narrow for the dogs, who could only stand around "crazed" with frustration while the chickens ate.) Mother said she had never imagined that Second Sister Yang could develop such speed on those little feet of hers.

My hometown receded ever farther into the distance and the familiar landscapes of the surrounding countryside gradually disappeared too. Strange to say, there was not a shred of regret in my heart. I only felt that there was a high and invisible wall all around me that isolated me from my fellow human beings, a wall that was squeezing the breath out of my body. That usually comforting image of a little hero with silver neckring standing in the middle of a melon patch was now blurred out of focus and stirred nothing in me but a feeling of melancholy.

Mother and Hong'er had both gone to sleep.

As I lay there and listened to the gentle slapping of water against the hull, I knew that Runtu and I were going on separate roads. "Even though we're irrevocably cut off from each other," I thought, "didn't Hong'er start to miss Shuisheng when we had barely set out? I hope they'll never live like my generation with everyone cut off from everyone else. And yet, just to keep that from happening, I wouldn't want them to have this vagabond life of mine, any more than I'd want them to have Runtu's barren one. Still less would I want them to muddle through the hedonistic lives other people lead. There ought to be a new life for them, a life that none of us has ever known."

As my thoughts turned toward hope, a feeling of anxiety suddenly possessed me. When Runtu took the censer and candlesticks, I had laughed at him behind his back. "Can't let go of that superstitious idol-worship of his for a single minute!" But what was this thing called "hope" if not an idol that *I* had fashioned with my own hands. The things he hoped for were immediate, while what I wanted was somewhere far off in the murky distance—that was the only difference.

As I lay there half asleep, an emerald-green plot of land by the sea appeared before my eyes. In the deep blue sky above it hung a moon, full and golden. "Hope isn't the kind of thing that you can say either exists or doesn't exist," I thought to myself. "It's like a path across the land—it's not there to begin with, but when lots of people go the same way, it comes into being."

Translated by William Lyell

Spring Silkworms

Mao Dun

I

OLD TONG BAO sat on a rock beside the road that skirted the canal, his long-stemmed pipe lying on the ground next to him. Though it was only a few days after the Qingming Festival the April sun was already very strong. It scorched Old Tong Bao's spine like a basin of fire. Straining down the road, the men towing the fast junk wore only thin

---

MAO DUN (1896–1981) spent his early career in the 1920s as an editor, introducing Western literary ideas, particularly naturalism, to Chinese readers. In the late 1920s, perhaps in reaction to the failure of the communist revolutionary movement with which he had become involved, he turned to fiction, writing first short stories—such as the one presented here—and later novels, most famously *Midnight* (1933), a depiction of capitalists in 1930s Shanghai. Though one can clearly find in it a political motive, "Spring Silkworms" is perhaps best seen as an endearing and sympathetic depiction of physical labor. The peasants in this story struggle to survive against the forces of nature and a global economic system of which they are completely ignorant. Written in 1932, the story resonates with the rural China of today, which is struggling with the forces of globalization.

---

tunics, open in front. They were bent far forward, pulling, pulling, pulling, great beads of sweat dripping from their brows.

The sight of others toiling strenuously made Old Tong Bao feel even warmer; he began to itch. He was still wearing the tattered padded jacket in which he had passed the winter. His unlined jacket had not yet been redeemed from the pawn shop. Who would have believed it could get so hot right after Qingming?

Even the weather's not what it used to be, Old Tong Bao said to himself, and spat emphatically.

Before him, the water of the canal was green and shiny. Occasional passing boats broke the mirror-smooth surface into ripples and eddies, turning the reflection of the earthen bank and the long line of mulberry trees flanking it into a dancing gray blur. But not for long! Gradually the trees reappeared, twisting and weaving drunkenly. Another few minutes, and they were again standing still, reflected as clearly as before. On the gnarled fists of the mulberry branches, little fingers of tender green buds were already bursting forth. Crowded close together, the trees along the canal seemed to march endlessly into the distance. The unplanted fields as yet were only cracked clods of dry earth; the mulberry trees reigned supreme here this time of the year! Behind Old Tong Bao's back was another great stretch of mulberry trees, squat, silent. The little buds seemed to be growing bigger every second in the hot sunlight.

Not far from where Old Tong Bao was sitting, a gray two-story building crouched beside the road. That was the silk filature, where the delicate fibers were removed from the cocoons. Two weeks ago it was occupied by troops; a few short trenches still scarred the fields around it. Everyone had said that the Japanese soldiers were attacking in this direction. The rich people in the market town had all run away. Now the troops were gone, and the silk filature stood empty and locked as before. There would be no noise and excitement in it again until cocoon-selling time.

Old Tong Bao had heard Young Master Chen—son of the Master Chen who lived in town—say that Shanghai was seething with unrest, that all the silk weaving factories had closed their doors, that the silk filatures here probably wouldn't open either. But he couldn't believe it. He had been through many periods of turmoil and strife in his sixty years, yet he had never seen a time when the shiny green mulberry leaves had been allowed to wither on the branches and become fodder for sheep. Of course, if the silkworm eggs shouldn't ripen, that would be different. Such matters were all in the hands of the Old Lord of the Sky. Who could foretell His will?

"Only just after Qingming and so hot already!" marveled Old Tong Bao, gazing at the small green mulberry leaves. He was happy as well as surprised. He could remember only one year when it was too hot for padded clothes at Qingming. He was in his twenties then, and the silkworm eggs had hatched "200 percent"! That was the year he got married. His family was flourishing in those days. His father was like an experienced plow ox—there was nothing he didn't understand, nothing he wasn't willing to try. Even his old grandfather—the one who had started the family on the road to prosperity—seemed to be growing more hearty with age, in spite of the hard time he was said to have had during the years he was a prisoner of the Long Hairs [of the Taiping Army].

Old Master Chen was still alive then. His son, the present Master Chen, hadn't begun smoking opium yet, and the House of Chen hadn't become the bad lot it was today. Moreover, even though the House of Chen was the rich gentry and his own family only ordinary tillers of the land, Old Tong Bao had felt that the destinies of the two families were linked together. Years ago, Long Hairs campaigning through the countryside had captured Tong Bao's grandfather and Old Master Chen and kept them working as prisoners for nearly seven years in the same camp. They had escaped together, taking a lot of the Long Hairs' gold with them—people still talk about it to this day. What's more, at the same time Old Master Chen's silk trade began to prosper, the cocoon raising of Tong Bao's family grew successful too. Within ten years Grandfather had earned enough to buy three acres of rice paddy and two acres of mulberry grove, and build a modest house. Tong Bao's family was the envy of the people of East Village, just as the House of Chen ranked among the first families in the market town.

But afterward both families had declined. Today, Old Tong Bao had no land of his own; in fact he was over three hundred silver dollars in debt. The House of Chen was finished too. People said the spirit of the dead Long Hairs had sued the Chens in the underworld, and because the King of Hell had decreed that the Chens repay the fortune they had amassed on the stolen gold, the family had gone down financially very quickly. Old Tong Bao was rather inclined to believe this. If it hadn't been for the influence of devils, why would a decent fellow like Master Chen have taken to smoking opium?

What Old Tong Bao could never understand was why the fall of the House of Chen should affect his own family. They certainly hadn't kept any of the Long Hairs' gold. True, his father had related that when Grandfather was escaping from the Long Hairs' camp he had run into a young Long Hair on patrol and had to kill him. What else could he have done? It was fate! Still from Tong Bao's earliest recollections, his family had prayed and offered sacrifices to appease the soul of the departed young Long Hair time and time again. That little wronged spirit should have left the nether world and been reborn long ago by now! Although Old Tong Bao couldn't recall what sort of man his grandfather was, he knew his father had been hardworking and honest—he had seen that with his own eyes. Old Tong Bao himself was a respectable person; both A Si, his elder son, and his daughter-in-law were industrious and frugal. Only his younger son, A Duo, was inclined to be a little flighty. But youngsters were all like that. There was nothing really bad about the boy.

Old Tong Bao raised his wrinkled face, scorched by years of hot sun to the color of dark parchment. He gazed bitterly at the canal before him, at the boats on its waters, at the mulberry trees along its banks. All were approximately the same as they had been when he was twenty. But the world had changed. His family now often had to make their meals of pumpkin instead of rice. He was over three hundred silver dollars in debt.

Toot! Toot-toot-toot . . .

Far up the bend in the canal a boat whistle broke the silence. There was a silk filature over there too. He could see vaguely the neat lines of stones embedded as a reinforcement in the canal bank. A small oil-burning river boat came puffing up pompously from beyond the silk filature, tugging three larger craft in its wake. Immediately the peaceful water was agitated with waves rolling toward the banks on both sides of the canal. A peasant, poling a tiny boat, hastened to shore and clutched a clump of reeds growing in the shallows. The waves tossed him and his little craft up and down like a seesaw. The peaceful green countryside was filled with the chugging of the boat engine and the stink of its exhaust.

Hatred burned in Old Tong Bao's eyes. He watched the riverboat approach, he watched it sail past, and glared after it until it went tooting around another bend and disappeared from sight. He had always abominated the foreign devils' contraptions. He himself had never met a foreign devil, but his father had given him a description of one Old Master Chen had seen—red eyebrows, green eyes, and a stiff-legged walk! Old Master Chen had hated the foreign devils too. "The foreign devils have swindled our money away," he used to say. Old Tong Bao was only eight or nine the last time he saw Old Master Chen. All he remembered about him now were things he had heard from others. But whenever Old Tong Bao thought of that remark—"The foreign devils have swindled our money away"—he could almost picture Old Master Chen, stroking his beard and wagging his head.

How the foreign devils had accomplished this, Old Tong Bao wasn't too clear. He was sure, however, that

Old Master Chen was right. Some things he himself had seen quite plainly. From the time foreign goods—cambric, cloth, oil—appeared in the market town, from the time foreign riverboats increased on the canal, what he produced brought a lower price on the market every day, while what he had to buy became more and more expensive. That was why the property his father left him had shrunk until it finally vanished completely; and now he was in debt. It was not without reason that Old Tong Bao hated the foreign devils!

In the village, his attitude toward foreigners was well known. Five years before, in 1927, someone had told him: "The new Guomindang government says it wants to throw out the foreign devils." Old Tong Bao didn't believe it. He had heard those young propaganda speechmakers the Guomindang sent when he went into the market town. Though they cried "Throw out the foreign devils," they were dressed in Western-style clothing. His guess was that they were secretly in league with the foreign devils, that they had been purposely sent to delude the country-folk! Sure enough, the Guomindang dropped the slogan not long after, and prices and taxes rose steadily. Old Tong Bao was firmly convinced that all this had occurred as part of a government conspiracy with the foreign devils.

Last year something had happened that made him almost sick with fury: only the cocoons spun by the foreign-strain silkworms could be sold at a decent price. Buyers paid ten dollars more per load for them than they did for the local variety. Usually on good terms with his daughter-in-law, Old Tong Bao had quarreled with her because of this. She had wanted to raise only foreign silkworms, and Old Tong Bao's younger son A Duo had agreed with her. Though the boy didn't say much, in his heart he certainly had also favored this course. Events had proved they were right, and they wouldn't let Old Tong Bao forget it. This year, he had to compromise. Of the five trays they would raise, only four would be silkworms of the local variety; one tray would contain foreign silkworms.

"The world's going from bad to worse! In another couple of years they'll even be wanting foreign mulberry trees! It's enough to take all the joy out of life!"

Old Tong Bao picked up his long pipe and rapped it angrily against a clod of dry earth. The sun was directly overhead now, foreshortening his shadow until it looked like a piece of charcoal. Still in his padded jacket, he was bathed in heat. He unfastened the jacket and swung its opened edges back and forth a few times to fan himself. Then he stood up and started for home.

Behind the row of mulberry trees were paddy fields. Most of them were as yet only neatly ploughed furrows of upturned earth clods, dried and cracked by the hot sun. Here and there, the early crops were coming up. In one field, the golden blossoms of rapeseed plants emitted a heady fragrance. And that group of houses way over there, that was the village where three generations of Old Tong Bao's family were living. Above the houses, white smoke from many kitchen stoves was curling lazily upward into the sky.

After crossing through the mulberry grove, Old Tong Bao walked along the raised path between the paddy fields, then turned and looked again at that row of trees bursting with tender green buds. A twelve-year-old boy came bounding along from the other end of the fields, calling as he ran:

"Grandpa! Ma's waiting for you to come home and eat!"

It was Little Bao, Old Tong Bao's grandson.

"Coming!" the old man responded, still gazing at the mulberries. Only twice in his life had he seen these finger-like buds appear on the branches so soon after Qingming. His family would probably have a fine crop of silkworms this year. Five trays of eggs would hatch out a huge number of silkworms. If only they didn't have another bad market like last year, perhaps they could pay off part of their debt.

Little Bao stood beside his grandfather. The child too looked at the soft green on the gnarled fist branches. Jumping happily, he clapped his hands and chanted:

> Green, tender leaves at Qingming;
> the girls who tend silkworms
> clap hands at the sight!

The old man's wrinkled face broke into a smile. He thought it was a good omen for the little boy to respond like this on seeing the first buds of the year. He rubbed his hand affectionately over the child's shaven pate. In Old Tong Bao's heart, numbed wooden by a lifetime of poverty and hardship, suddenly hope began to stir again.

2

The weather remained warm. The rays of the sun forced open the tender, fingerlike little buds. They had already grown to the size of a small hand. Around Old Tong

Bao's village, the mulberry trees seemed to respond especially well. From a distance they gave the appearance of
a low gray picket fence on top of which a long swath of
brocade had been spread. Bit by bit, day by day, hope grew
in the hearts of the villagers. The unspoken mobilization
order for the silkworm campaign reached everywhere and
everyone. Silkworm rearing equipment that had been laid
away for a year was again brought out to be scrubbed and
mended. Beside the little stream which ran through the
village, women and children, with much laughter and
calling back and forth, washed the implements.

None of these women or children looked really healthy.
Since the coming of spring, they had been eating only
half their fill; their clothes were old and worn. As a matter of fact, they weren't much better off than beggars.
Yet all were in quite good spirits, sustained by enormous
patience and grand illusions. Burdened though they were
by daily mounting debts, they had only one thought in
their heads—if we get a good crop of silkworms everything will be all right! . . . They could already visualize
how, in a month, the shiny green leaves would be converted into snow-white cocoons, the cocoons exchanged
for clinking silver dollars. Although their stomachs were
growling with hunger, they couldn't refrain from smiling
at this happy prospect.

Old Tong Bao's daughter-in-law was among the women
by the stream. With the help of her twelve-year-old son,
Little Bao, she had already finished washing the family's
large trays of woven bamboo strips. Seated on a stone
beside the stream, she wiped her perspiring face with the
edge of her tunic. A twenty-year-old girl working with

other women on the opposite side of the stream, hailed her.

"Are you raising foreign silkworms this year too?"

It was Sixth Treasure, sister of young Fuqing, the neighbor who lived across the stream.

The thick eyebrows of Old Tong Bao's daughter-in-law at once contracted. Her voice sounded as if she had just been waiting for a chance to let off steam.

"Don't ask me; what the old man says, goes!" she shouted. "He's dead set against it, won't let us raise more than one batch of foreign breed! The old fool only has to hear the word *foreign* to send him up in the air! He'll take dollars made of foreign silver, though; those are the only 'foreign' things he likes!"

The women on the other side of the stream laughed. From the threshing ground behind them a strapping young man approached. He reached the stream and crossed over on the four logs that served as a bridge. Seeing him, his sister-in-law dropped her tirade and called in a high voice:

"A Duo, will you help me carry these trays? They're as heavy as dead dogs when they're wet!"

Without a word, A Duo lifted the six big trays and set them, dripping, on his head. Balancing them in place, he walked off, swinging his hands in a swimming motion. When in a good mood, A Duo refused nobody. If any of the village women asked him to carry something heavy or fish something out of the stream, he was usually quite willing. But today he probably was a little grumpy, and so he walked empty-handed with only six trays on his head. The sight of him, looking as if he were wearing six layers of wide straw hats, his waist twisting at each step in imitation of the ladies of the town, sent the women into peals of laughter. Lotus, wife of Old Tong Bao's nearest neighbor, called with a giggle:

"Hey, A Duo, come back here. Carry a few trays for me too!"

A Duo grinned, "Not unless you call me a sweet name!" He continued walking. An instant later he had reached the porch of his house and set down the trays out of the sun.

"Will 'kid brother' do?" demanded Lotus, laughing boisterously. She had a remarkably clean white complexion, but her face was very flat. When she laughed, all that could be seen was a big open mouth and two tiny slits of eyes. Originally a maid in a house in town, she had been married off to Old Tong Bao's neighbor—a prematurely aged man who walked around with a sour expression and never said a word all day. That was less than six months ago, but her love affairs and escapades already were the talk of the village.

"Shameless hussy!" came a contemptuous female voice from across the stream.

Lotus's piggy eyes immediately widened. "Who said that?" she demanded angrily. If you've got the brass to call me names, let's see you try it to my face! Come out into the open!"

"Think you can handle me? I'm talking about a shameless, man-crazy baggage! If the shoe fits, wear it!" retorted Sixth Treasure, for it was she who had spoken. She too was famous in the village, but as a mischievous, lively young woman.

The two began splashing water at each other from opposite banks of the stream. Girls who enjoyed a row took sides and joined the battle, while the children whooped with laughter. Old Tong Bao's daughter-in-law was more decorous. She picked up her remaining trays, called to Little Bao, and returned home. A Duo watched from the porch, grinning. He knew why Sixth Treasure and Lotus were quarreling. It did his heart good to hear that sharp-tongued Sixth Treasure get told off in public.

Old Tong Bao came out of the house with a wooden tray-stand on his shoulder. Some of the legs of the uprights had been eaten by termites, and he wanted to repair them. At the sight of A Duo standing there laughing at the women, Old Tong Bao's face lengthened. The boy hadn't much sense of propriety, he well knew. What disturbed him particularly was the way A Duo and Lotus were always talking and laughing together. "That bitch is an evil spirit. Fooling with her will bring ruin on our house," he had often warned his younger son,

"A Duo!" he now barked angrily. "Enjoying the scenery? Your brother's in back mending equipment. Go and give him a hand!" His inflamed eyes bored into A Duo, never leaving the boy until he disappeared into the house. Only then did Old Tong Bao start work on the tray-stand. After examining it carefully, he slowly began his repairs. Years ago, Old Tong Bao had worked for a time as a carpenter. But he was old now; his fingers had lost their strength. A few minutes' work and he was breathing hard. He raised his head and looked into the house. Five squares of cloth to which sticky silkworm eggs adhered hung from a horizontal bamboo pole.

His daughter-in-law, A Si's wife, was at the other end of the porch, pasting paper on big trays of woven bamboo strips. Last year, to economize a bit, they had bought and used old newspaper. Old Tong Bao still maintained that was why the eggs had hatched poorly—it was unlucky to use paper with writing on it for such a prosaic purpose. Writing meant scholarship, and scholarship had to be respected. This year the whole family had skipped a meal and, with the money saved, purchased special "tray pasting paper." A Si's wife pasted the tough, gosling-yellow sheets smooth and flat; on every tray she also affixed three little colored paper pictures bought at the same time. One was the "Platter of Plenty"; the other two showed a militant figure on horseback, pennant in hand. He, according to local belief, was the "Guardian of Silkworm Hatching."

"I was only able to buy twenty loads of mulberry leaves with that thirty silver dollars I borrowed on your father's guarantee," Old Tong Bao said to his daughter-in-law. He was still panting from his exertions with the tray-stand. "Our rice will be finished by the day after tomorrow. What are we going to do?" Thanks to her father's influence with his boss and his willingness to guarantee repayment of the loan, Old Tong Bao was able to borrow money at a low rate of interest—only 25 percent a month! Both the principal and interest had to be repaid by the end of the silkworm season.

A Si's wife finished pasting a tray and placed it in the sun. "You've spent it all on leaves," she said angrily. "We'll have a lot of leaves left over, just like last year!"

"Full of lucky words, aren't you?" demanded the old man sarcastically. "I suppose every year'll be like last year?

We can't get more than a dozen or so loads of leaves from our own trees. With five sets of grubs to feed, that won't be nearly enough."

"Oh, of course, you're never wrong!" she replied hotly. "All know is with rice we can eat, without it we'll go hungry!" His stubborn refusal to raise any foreign silkworms last year had left them with only the unsalable local breed. As a result, she was often contrary with him.

The old man's face turned purple with rage. After this, neither would speak to the other.

But hatching time was drawing closer every day. The little village's two dozen families were thrown into a state of great tension, great determination, great struggle. With it all, they were possessed of a great hope, a hope that could almost make them forget their hungry bellies.

Old Tong Bao's family, borrowing a little here, getting a little credit there, somehow managed to get by. Nor did the other families eat any better: there wasn't one with a spare bag of rice. Although they had harvested a good crop the previous year, landlords, creditors, taxes, levies, one after another, had cleaned the peasants out long ago. Now all their hopes were pinned on the spring silkworms. The repayment date of every load they made was set up for the "end of the silkworm season."

With high hopes and considerable fear, like soldiers going into hand-to-hand combat, they prepared for the silkworm campaign!

"Grain Rain" day-bringing gentle drizzles—was not far off. Almost imperceptibly, the silkworm eggs of the two dozen village families began to show faint tinges of green. Women, when they met on the public threshing ground, would speak to one another agitatedly in tones that were anxious yet joyful.

"Over at Sixth Treasure's place, they're almost ready to incubate their eggs!"

"Lotus says her family is going to start incubating tomorrow. So soon!"

"Huang 'the Priest' has made a divination. He predicts that this spring mulberry leaves will go to four dollars a load!"

Old Tong Bao's daughter-in-law examined their five sets of eggs. They looked bad. The tiny seed-like eggs were still pitch black, without even a hint of green. Her husband, A Si, took them into the light to peer at them carefully. Even so, he could find hardly any ripening eggs. She was very worried.

"You incubate them anyhow. Maybe this variety is a little slow, " her husband forced himself to say consolingly.

Her lips pressed tight, she made no reply.

Old Tong Bao's wrinkled face sagged with dejection. Though he said nothing, he thought their prospects were dim.

The next day, A Si's wife again examined the eggs. Ha! Quite a few were turning green, and a very shiny green at that! Immediately, she told her husband, told Old Tong Bao, A Duo . . . she even told her son Little Bao. Now the incubating process could begin! She held the five pieces of cloth to which the eggs adhered against her bare bosom. As if cuddling a nursing infant, she sat absolutely quiet, not daring to stir. At night, she took the five sets to bed with her. Her husband was routed out, and had to share A Duo's bed. The tiny silkworm eggs were very scratchy against her flesh. She felt happy and a little frightened, like the first time she was pregnant and the baby moved inside her. Exactly the same sensation!

Uneasy but eager, the whole family waited for the eggs to hatch. A Duo was the only exception. "We're sure going to hatch a good crop," he said, "but anyone who thinks we're going to get rich in this life is out of his head." Though the old man swore A Duo's big mouth would ruin their luck, the boy stuck to his guns.

A clean, dry shed for the growing grubs was all prepared. The second day of incubation, Old Tong Bao smeared a garlic with earth and placed it at the foot of the wall inside the shed. If, in a few days, the garlic put out many sprouts, it meant the eggs would hatch well. He did this every year, but this year he was more reverential than usual, and his hands trembled. Last year's divination had proved all too accurate. He didn't dare to think about that now.

Every family in the village was busy incubating. For the time being there were few women's footprints on the threshing ground or the banks of the little stream. An unofficial "martial law" had been imposed. Even peasants normally on very good terms stopped visiting one another. For a guest to come and frighten away the spirits of the ripening eggs-that would be no laughing matter! At most, people exchanged a few words in low tones when they met, then quickly separated. This was the "sacred" season!

Old Tong Bao's family was on pins and needles. In the five sets of eggs a few grubs had begun wriggling. It was exactly one day before Grain Rain. A Si's wife had calculated that most of the eggs wouldn't hatch until after that day. Before or after Grain Rain was all right, but for eggs to hatch on the day itself was considered highly unlucky. Incubation was no longer necessary, and the eggs were carefully placed in the special shed. Old Tong Bao stole a glance at his garlic at the foot of the wall. His heart dropped. There were still only the same two small green shoots the garlic had originally! He didn't dare to look any closer. He prayed silently that by noon the day after tomorrow the garlic would have many, many more shoots.

At last hatching day arrived. A Si's wife set a pot of rice on to boil and nervously watched for the time when the steam from it would rise straight up. Old Tong Bao lit the incense and candles he had bought in anticipation of this event. Devoutly, he placed them before the idol of the Kitchen God. His two sons went into the fields to pick wildflowers. Little Bao chopped a lamp wick into fine pieces and crushed the wildflowers the men brought back. Everything was ready. The sun was entering its zenith; steam from the rice pot puffed straight upward. A Si's wife immediately leaped to her feet, stuck a "sacred" paper flower and a pair of goose feathers into the knot of hair at the back of her head, and went to the shed. Old Tong Bao carried a wooden scale-pole; A Si followed with the chopped lamp wick and the crushed wildflowers. Daughter-in-law uncovered the cloth pieces to which the grubs adhered, and sprinkled them with the bits of wick and flowers A Si was holding. Then she took the wooden scale-pole from Old Tong Bao and hung the cloth pieces over it. She next removed the pair of goose feathers from her hair. Moving them lightly across the cloth, she brushed the grubs, together with the crushed lamp-wick and wildflowers, onto a large tray. One set, two sets . . . the last set contained the foreign breed. The grubs from this cloth were brushed onto a separate tray. Finally, she removed the "sacred" paper flower from her hair and pinned it, with the goose feathers, against the side of the tray.

A solemn ceremony! One that had been handed down through the ages! Like warriors taking an oath before going into battle! Old Tong Bao and family now had ahead of them a month of fierce combat, with no rest day or night, against bad weather, bad luck, and anything else that might come along!

The grubs, wriggling in the trays, looked very healthy. They were all the proper black color. Old Tong Bao and his daughter-in-law were able to relax a little. But when the old man secretly took another look at his garlic, he turned pale! It had grown only four measly shoots. Ah! Would this year be like last year all over again?

3

The fateful garlic proved to be not so psychic after all. The silkworms of Old Tong Bao's family grew and thrived! Though it rained continuously during the grubs' first and second molting, and the weather was a bit colder than at Qingming, the "little darlings" were extremely robust. The silkworms of the other families in the village were not doing so badly either. A tense kind of joy pervaded the countryside. Even the small stream seemed to be gurgling with bright laughter. Lotus's family was the sole exception. They were only raising one set of grubs, but by the third molting their silkworms weighed less than twenty catties. Just before the fourth, people saw Lotus's husband walk to the stream and dump out his trays. That dour, old-looking man had bad luck written all over him. Because of this dreadful event, the village women put Lotus's family strictly off limits. They made wide detours so as not to pass her door. If they saw her or her taciturn husband, no matter how far away, they made haste to go in the opposite direction. They feared that even one look at Lotus or her spouse, the briefest conversation, would contaminate them with the unfortunate couple's bad luck!

Old Tong Bao strictly forbade A Duo to talk to Lotus. "If I catch you gabbing with that baggage again, I'll disown you!" he threatened in a loud, angry voice, standing outside on the porch to make sure Lotus could hear him.

Little Bao was also warned not to play in front of Lotus's door, and not to speak to anyone in her family.

The old man harped at A Duo morning, noon, and night, but the boy turned a deaf ear to his father's grumbling. In his heart, he laughed at it. Of the whole family, A Duo alone didn't place much stock in taboos and superstitions. He didn't talk with Lotus, however. He was much too busy for that.

By the fourth molting, their silkworms weighed three hundred catties. Every member of Old Tong Bao's family, including twelve-year-old Little Bao, worked for two days and two nights without sleeping a wink. The silkworms were unusually sturdy. Only twice in his sixty years had Old Tong Bao ever seen the like. Once was the year he married; once when his first son was born.

The first day after the fourth molting, the "little darlings" ate seven loads of leaves. They were now a bright
green, thick and healthy. Old Tong Bao and his family,
on the contrary, were much thinner, their eyes bloodshot
from lack of sleep.

No one could guess how much the "little darlings"
would eat before they spun their cocoons. Old Tong Bao
discussed the question of buying more leaves with A Si.

"Master Chen won't lend us any more. Shall we try
your father-in-law's boss again?"

"We've still got ten loads coming. That's enough for
one more day," replied A Si. He could barely hold himself
erect. His eyelids weighed a thousand catties. They kept
wanting to close.

"One more day? You're dreaming!" snapped the old
man impatiently. "Not counting tomorrow, they still have
to eat three more days. We'll need another thirty loads!
Thirty loads, I say!"

Loud voices were heard outside on the threshing
ground. A Duo had arrived with men delivering five
loads of mulberry branches. Everyone went out to strip
the leaves. A Si's wife hurried from the shed. Across the
stream, Sixth Treasure and her family were raising only
a small crop of silkworms; having spare time, she came
over to help. Bright stars filled the sky. There was a slight
wind. All up and down the village, gay shouts and laughter rang in the night.

"The price of leaves is rising fast!" a coarse voice cried.
"This afternoon, they were getting four dollars a load in
the market town!" Old Tong Bao was very upset. At four
dollars a load, thirty loads would come to a hundred and

twenty dollars. Where could he raise so much money?! But then he figured—he was sure to gather over five hundred catties of cocoons. Even at fifty dollars a hundred, they'd sell for two hundred and fifty dollars. Feeling a bit consoled, he heard a small voice from among the leaf-strippers.

"They say the folks east of here aren't doing so well with their silkworms. There won't be any reason for the price of leaves to go much higher."

Old Tong Bao recognized the speaker as Sixth Treasure, and he relaxed still further.

The girl and A Duo were standing beside a large basket, stripping leaves. In the dim starlight, they worked quite close to each other, partly hidden by the pile of mulberry branches before them. Suddenly Sixth Treasure felt someone pinch her thigh. She knew well enough who it was, and she suppressed a giggle. But when, a moment later, a hand brushed against her breasts, she jumped; a little shriek escaped her.

"*Ai-ya!*"

"What's wrong?" demanded A Si's wife, working on the other side of the basket.

Sixth Treasure's face flamed scarlet. She shot a glance at A Duo, then quickly lowered her head and resumed stripping leaves. "Nothing," she replied. "I think a caterpillar bit me!"

A Duo bit his lips to keep from laughing aloud. He had been half starved the past two weeks and had slept little. But in spite of having lost a lot of weight, he was in high spirits. While he never suffered from any of Old Tong Bao's gloom, neither did he believe that one good crop, whether of silkworms or of rice, would enable them to wipe out their debt and own their own land again. He knew that they would never get out from under merely by relying on hard work, even if they broke their backs trying. Nevertheless, he worked with a will. He enjoyed work, just as he enjoyed fooling around with Sixth Treasure. The next morning, Old Tong Bao went into town to borrow money for more leaves. Before leaving home, he had talked the matter over with daughter-in-law. They had decided to mortgage their grove of mulberries that produced fifteen loads of leaves a year as security for the loan. The grove was the last piece of property the family owned.

By the time the old man ordered another thirty loads and the first ten were delivered, the sturdy "little darlings" had gone hungry for half an hour. Putting forth their pointed little mouths, they swayed from side to side, searching for food. Daughter-in-law's heart had ached to see them. When the leaves were finally spread on the trays, the silkworm shed at once resounded with a sibilant crunching, so noisy it drowned out conversation. In a very short while, the trays were again empty of leaves. Another thick layer was piled on. Just keeping the silkworms supplied with leaves, Old Tong Bao and his family were so busy they could barely catch their breath. But this was the final crisis. In two more days the "little darlings" would spin their cocoons. People were putting every bit of their remaining strength into this last desperate struggle.

Though he had gone without sleep for three whole days, A Duo didn't appear particularly tired. He agreed to watch the shed alone that night until dawn to permit the others to get some rest. There was a bright moon, and the weather was a trifle cold. A Duo crouched beside a small fire he had built in the shed. At about eleven, he gave the silkworms their second feeding, then returned to squat by the fire. He could hear the loud rustle of the "little darlings" crunching through the leaves. His eyes closed. Suddenly he heard the door squeak, and his eyelids flew open. He peered into the darkness for a moment, then shut his eyes again. His ears were still hissing with the rustle of the leaves. The next thing he knew, his head had struck against his knees. Waiting with a start, he heard the door screen bang and thought he saw a moving shadow. A Duo leaped up and rushed outside. In the moonlight, he saw someone crossing the threshing ground toward the stream. He caught up in a flash, seized and flung the intruder to the ground. A Duo was sure he had nabbed a thief.

"A Duo, kill me if you want to, but don't give me away!"

The voice made A Duo's hair stand on end. He could see in the moonlight that queer, flat, white face and those round little piggy eyes fixed upon him. But of menace, the piggy eyes had none. A Duo snorted.

"What were you after?"

"A few of your family's 'little darlings'!"

"What did you do with them?"

"Threw them in the stream!"

A Duo's face darkened. He knew that in this way she was trying to put a curse on the lot. "You're pure poison! We never did anything to hurt you."

"Never did anything? Oh, yes you did! Yes, you did! Our silkworm eggs didn't hatch well, but we didn't harm anybody. You were all so smart! You shunned me like a leper. No matter how far away I was, if you saw me you turned your heads. You acted as if I wasn't even human!"

She got to her feet, the agonized expression on her face terrible to see. A Duo stared at her. "I'm not going to beat you," he said finally. "Go on your way!"

Without giving her another glance, he trotted back to the shed. He was wide awake now. Lotus had only taken a handful, and the remaining "little darlings" were all in good condition. It didn't occur to him to either hate or pity Lotus, but the last thing she had said remained in his mind. It seemed to him there was something eternally wrong in the scheme of human relations; but he couldn't put his finger on what it was exactly, nor did he know why it should be. In a little while, he forgot about this too. The lusty silkworms were eating and eating, yet, as if by some magic, never full! But when, at sunrise, A Si's wife went to draw water at the stream, she met Sixth Treasure. The girl's expression was serious.

"I saw that slut leaving your place shortly before midnight," she whispered. "A Duo was right behind her. They stood here and talked for a long time! Your family ought to look after things better than that!"

The color drained from the face of A Si's wife. Without a word, she carried her water bucket back to the house. First she told her husband about it, then she told Old Tong Bao. It was a fine state of affairs when a baggage like that could sneak into people's silkworm sheds! Old Tong Bao stamped with rage. He immediately summoned A Duo. But the boy denied the whole story; he said Sixth Treasure was dreaming. The old man then went to question Sixth Treasure. She insisted she had seen everything with her own eyes. The old man didn't know what to believe. He returned home and looked at the "little darlings." They were as sturdy as ever, not a sickly one in the lot.

But the joy that Old Tong Bao and his family had been feeling was dampened. They knew Sixth Treasure's words couldn't be entirely without foundation. Their only hope was that A Duo and that hussy had played their little games on the porch rather than in the shed!

Old Tong Bao recalled gloomily that the garlic had only put forth three or four shoots. He thought the future looked dark.

Hadn't there been times before when the silkworms ate great quantities of leaves and seemed to be growing well, yet dried up and died just when they were ready to spin their cocoons? Yes, often! But Old Tong Bao didn't dare let himself think of such a possibility. To entertain a thought like that, even in the most secret recesses of the mind, would only be inviting bad luck!

4

The "little darlings" began spinning their cocoons, but Old Tong Bao's family was still in a sweat. Both their money and their energy were completely spent. They still had nothing to show for it; there was no guarantee of their earning any return. Nevertheless, they continued working at top speed. Beneath the racks on which the cocoons were being spun, fires had to be kept going to supply warmth. Old Tong Bao and A Si, his elder son, their backs bent, slowly squatted first on this side and then on that. Hearing the small rustlings of the spinning silkworms, they wanted to smile, and if the sounds stopped for a moment, their hearts stopped too. Yet, worried as they were, they didn't dare disturb the silkworms by looking inside. When the silkworms squirted fluid in their faces as they peered up from beneath the racks, they were quite happy in spite of the momentary discomfort. The bigger the shower, the better they liked it.

A Duo had already peeked several times. Little Bao had caught him at it and demanded to know what was going on. A Duo made an ugly face at the child, but did not reply.

After three days of "spinning," the fires were extinguished. A Si's wife could restrain herself no longer. She stole a look, her heart beating fast. Inside, all was as white as snow. The brush that had been put in for the silkworms to spin on was completely covered over with cocoons. A Si's wife had never seen so successful a "flowering"!

The whole family was wreathed in smiles. They were on solid ground at last! The "little darlings" had proved they had a conscience; they hadn't consumed those mulberry leaves, at four dollars a load, in vain. The family could reap its reward for a month of hunger and sleepless nights. The Old Lord of the Sky had eyes!

Throughout the village, there were many similar scenes of rejoicing. The Silkworm Goddess had been beneficent to the tiny village this year. Most of the two dozen families garnered good crops of cocoons from their silkworms. The harvest of Old Tong Bao's family was well above average.

Again women and children crowded the threshing

ground and the banks of the little stream. All were much thinner than the previous month, with eyes sunk in their sockets, throats rasping and hoarse. But everyone was excited, happy. As they chattered about the struggle of the past month, visions of piles of bright silver dollars shimmered before their eyes. Cheerful thoughts filled their minds—they would get their summer clothes out of the pawnshop; at Summer Festival perhaps they could eat a fat, golden fish . . .

They talked too of the farce enacted by Lotus and A Duo a few nights before. Sixth Treasure announced to everyone she met, "That Lotus has no shame at all. She delivered herself right to his door!" Men who heard her laughed coarsely. Women muttered a prayer and called Lotus bad names. They said Old Tong Bao's family could consider itself lucky that a curse hadn't fallen on them. The gods were merciful!

Family after family was able to report a good harvest of cocoons. People visited one another to view the shining white gossamer. The father of Old Tong Bao's daughter-in-law came from town with his little son. They brought gifts of sweets and fruits and a salted fish. Little Bao was happy as a puppy frolicking in the snow.

The elderly visitor sat with Old Tong Bao beneath a willow beside the stream. He had the reputation in town of a "man who knew how to enjoy life." From hours of listening to the professional storytellers in front of the temple, he had learned by heart many of the classic tales of ancient times. He was a great one for idle chatter, and often would say anything that came into his head. Old Tong Bao therefore didn't take him very seriously when he leaned close and queried softly:

"Are you selling your cocoons, or will you spin the silk yourself at home?"

"Selling them, of course," Old Tong Bao replied casually.

The elderly visitor slapped his thigh and sighed, then rose abruptly and pointed at the silk filature rearing up behind the row of mulberries, now quite bald of leaves.

"Tong Bao," he said, "the cocoons are being gathered, but the doors of the silk filatures are shut as tight as ever! They're not buying this year! Ah, the world is in turmoil! The silk houses are not going to open, I tell you!"

Old Tong Bao couldn't help smiling. He wouldn't believe it. How could he possibly believe it? There were dozens of silk filatures in this part of the country. Surely they couldn't all shut down? What's more, he had heard that they had made a deal with the Japanese; the Chinese soldiers who had been billeted in the silk houses had long since departed.

Changing the subject, the visitor related the latest town gossip, salting it freely with classical aphorisms and quotations from the ancient stories. Finally he got around to the thirty silver dollars borrowed through him as middleman. He said his boss was anxious to be repaid.

Old Tong Bao became uneasy after all. When his visitor had departed, he hurried from the village down the highway to look at the two nearest silk filatures. Their doors were indeed shut; not a soul was in sight. Business was in full swing this time last year, with whole rows of dark gleaming scales in operation.

He felt a little panicky as he returned home. But when he saw those snowy cocoons, thick and hard, pleasure made him smile. What beauties! No one wants them?

Impossible. He still had to hurry and finish gathering the cocoons; he hadn't thanked the gods properly yet. Gradually, he forgot about the silk houses.

But in the village, the atmosphere was changing day by day. People who had just begun to laugh were now all frowns. News was reaching them from town that none of the neighboring silk filatures was opening its doors. It was the same with the houses along the highway. Last year at this time, buyers of cocoons were streaming in and out of the village. This year there wasn't a sign of even half a one. In their place came dunning creditors and government tax collectors who promptly froze up if you asked them to take cocoons in payment.

Swearing, curses, disappointed sighs! With such a fine crop of cocoons the villagers had never dreamed that their lot would be even worse than usual! It was as if hailstones had dropped out of a clear sky. People like Old Tong Bao, whose crop was especially good, took it hardest of all.

"What is the world coming to?" He beat his breast and stamped his feet in helpless frustration.

But the villagers had to think of something. The cocoons would spoil if kept too long. They either had to sell them or remove the silk themselves. Several families had already brought out and repaired silk reels they hadn't used for years. They would first remove the silk from the cocoons and then see about the next step. Old Tong Bao wanted to do the same.

"We don't sell our cocoons; we'll spin the silk ourselves!" said the old man. "Nobody ever heard of selling cocoons until the foreign devils' companies started the thing!"

A Si's wife was the first to object. "We've got over five

hundred catties of cocoons here," she retorted. "Where are you going to get enough reels?" She was right. Five hundred catties was no small amount. They'd never get finished spinning the silk themselves. Hire outside help? That meant spending money. A Si agreed with his wife. A Duo blamed his father for planning incorrectly.

"If you listened to me, we'd have raised only one tray of foreign breed and no locals. Then the fifteen loads of leaves from our own mulberry tree would have been enough, and we wouldn't have had to borrow!"

Old Tong Bao was so angry he couldn't speak.

At last a ray of hope appeared. Huang the Priest had heard somewhere that a silk house below the city of Wuxi was doing business as usual. Actually an ordinary peasant, Huang was nicknamed "The Priest" because of the learned airs he affected and his interest in Taoist "magic." Old Tong Bao always got along with him fine. After learning the details from him, Old Tong Bao conferred with his elder son A Si about going to Wuxi.

"It's about two hundred and seventy li by water, six days for the round trip," ranted the old man. "Son-of-a-bitch! It's a goddamn expedition! But what else can we do? We can't eat the cocoons, and our creditors are pressing hard!"

A Si agreed. They borrowed a small boat and bought a few yards of matting to cover the cargo. It was decided that A Duo should go along. Taking advantage of the good weather, the cocoon selling "expeditionary force" set out.

Five days later, the men returned—but not with an empty hold. They still had one basket of cocoons. The silk filature, which they reached after a journey of two hundred and seventy li by water, offered extremely harsh terms—only thirty-five dollars a load for foreign breed, twenty for local; thin cocoons not wanted at any price. Although their cocoons were all first class, the people at the silk filature house picked and chose only enough to fill one basket; the rest were rejected. Old Tong Bao and his sons received a hundred and ten dollars for the sale, ten of which had to be spent on travel expenses. The hundred dollars remaining was not even enough to pay back what they had borrowed for that last thirty loads of mulberry leaves! On the return trip, Old Tong Bao became ill with rage. His sons carried him into the house.

A Si's wife had no choice but to take the ninety odd catties they had brought back and reel the silk from the cocoons herself. She borrowed a few reels from Sixth Treasure's family and worked for six days. All their rice was gone now. A Si took the silk into town, but no one would buy it. Even the pawnshop didn't want it. Only after much pleading was he able to persuade the pawnbroker to take it in exchange for a load of rice they had pawned before Qingming.

That's the way it happened. Because they raised a crop of spring silkworms, the people in Old Tong Bao's village got deeper into debt. Old Tong Bao's family raised five trays and gathered a splendid harvest of cocoons. Yet they ended up owing another thirty silver dollars and losing their mortgaged mulberry trees—to say nothing of suffering a month of hunger and sleepless nights in vain!

Translated by Sidney Shapiro

Sealed Off
Zhang Ailing

THE TRAMCAR DRIVER drove his tram. The tram-car tracks, in the blazing sun, shimmered like two shiny eels crawling out of the water; they stretched and shrank, stretched and shrank, on their onward way—soft and slippery, long old eels, never ending, never ending . . . the driver fixed his eyes on the undulating tracks, and didn't go mad.

ZHANG AILING (Eileen Chang) (1920–95) was born in Shanghai and wrote mostly about the city of her birth. During the war in the 1940s she attended university in Hong Kong, and some of her fiction describes the ties that bind that city to her native Shanghai. In 1949 Zhang fled the mainland for Hong Kong and then the United States, where she spent the rest of her life as a virtual recluse, though she continued to write—and rewrite earlier works. Zhang's best works are the stories written in the 1940s and included in the collection *Legends* (1944). "Sealed Off," written in 1943, takes place during a Japanese air raid, when the city is under a blockade. It both paints a broad canvas of Shanghai's social classes and presents an intricate psychological portrait of an amorous relationship in the making. A writer who defies easy classification, Zhang wrote in a style uniquely her own that has modernist elements side-by-side with elements of contemporary urban entertainment fiction.

If there hadn't been an air raid, if the city hadn't been sealed, the tramcar would have gone on forever. The city was sealed. The alarm-bell rang. Ding-ding-ding-ding. Every "ding" was a cold little dot, the dots all adding up to a dotted line, cutting across time and space.

The tramcar ground to a halt, but the people on the street ran: those on the left side of the street ran over to the right, and those on the right ran over to the left. All the shops, in a single sweep, rattled down their metal gates. Matrons tugged madly at the railings. "Let us in for just a while," they cried. "We have children here, and old people!" But the gates stayed tightly shut. Those inside the metal gates and those outside the metal gates stood glaring at each other, fearing one another.

Inside the tram, people were fairly quiet. They had somewhere to sit, and though the place was rather plain, it still was better, for most of them, than what they had at home. Gradually, the street also grew quiet: not that it was a complete silence, but the sound of voices eased into a confused blur, like the soft rustle of a straw-stuffed pillow, heard in a dream. The huge, shambling city sat dozing in the sun, its head resting heavily on people's shoulders, its spittle slowly dripping down their shirts, an inconceivably enormous weight pressing down on everyone. Never before, it seemed, had Shanghai been this quiet—and in the middle of the day! A beggar, taking advantage of the breathless, birdless quiet, lifted up his voice and began to chant: "Good master, good lady, kind sir, kind ma'am, won't you give alms to this poor man? Good master, good lady . . ." But after a short while he stopped, scared silent by the eerie quiet.

Then there was a braver beggar, a man from Shandong, who firmly broke the silence. His voice was round and resonant: "Sad, sad, sad! No money do I have!" An old, old song, sung from one century to the next. The tram driver, who also was from Shandong, succumbed to the sonorous tune. Heaving a long sigh, he folded his arms across his chest, leaned against the tram door, and joined in: "Sad, sad, sad! No money do I have!"

Some of the tram passengers got out. But there was still a little loose, scattered chatter; near the door, a group of office workers was discussing something. One of them, with a quick, ripping sound, shook his fan open and offered his conclusion: "Well, in the end, there's nothing wrong with him—it's just that he doesn't know how to act." From another nose came a short grunt, followed by a cold smile: "Doesn't know how to act? He sure knows how to toady up to the bosses!"

A middle-aged couple who looked very much like brother and sister stood together in the middle of the tram, holding on to the leather straps. "Careful!" the woman suddenly yelped. "Don't get your trousers dirty!" The man flinched, then slowly raised the hand from which a packet of smoked fish dangled. Very cautiously, very gingerly, he held the paper packet, which was brimming with oil, several inches away from his suit pants. His wife did not let up. "Do you know what dry-cleaning costs these days? Or what it costs to get a pair of trousers made?"

Lu Zongzhen, accountant for Huamao Bank, was sitting in the corner. When he saw the smoked fish, he was reminded of the steamed dumplings stuffed with spinach that his wife had asked him to buy at a noodle stand near the bank. Women are always like that. Dumplings bought in the hardest-to-find, most twisty-windy little alleys had to be the best, no matter what. She didn't for a moment think of how it would be for him—neatly dressed in suit and tie, with tortoiseshell eyeglasses and a leather briefcase, then, tucked under his arm, these steaming hot dumplings wrapped in newspaper—how ludicrous! Still, if the city were sealed for a long time, so that his dinner was delayed, then he could at least make do with the dumplings.

He glanced at his watch; only four-thirty. Must be the power of suggestion. He felt hungry already. Carefully pulling back a corner of the paper, he took a look inside. Snowy white mounds, breathing soft little whiffs of sesame oil. A piece of newspaper had stuck to the dumplings, and he gravely peeled it off; the ink was printed on the dumplings, with all the writing in reverse, as though it were reflected in a mirror. He peered down and slowly picked the words out: "Obituaries . . . Positions Wanted . . . Stock Market Developments . . . Now Playing. . . ." Normal, useful phrases, but they did look a bit odd on a dumpling. Maybe because eating is such serious business; compared to it, everything else is just a joke. Lu Zongzhen thought it looked funny, but he didn't laugh: he was a very straightforward kind of fellow. After reading the dumplings, he read the newspaper, but when he'd finished half a page of old news, he found that if he turned the page all the dumplings would fall out, and so he had to stop.

While Lu read the paper, others in the tram did likewise. People who had newspapers read them; those with-

out newspapers read receipts, or lists of rules and regula-
tions, or business cards. People who were stuck without a
single scrap of printed matter read shop signs along the
street. They simply had to fill this terrifying emptiness—
otherwise, their brains might start to work. Thinking is a
painful business.

Sitting across from Lu Zongzhen was an old man
who, with a dull clacking sound, rolled two slippery,
glossy walnuts in his palm: a rhythmic little gesture can
substitute for thought. The old man had a clean-shaven
pate, a reddish yellow complexion, and an oily sheen on
his face. When his brows were furrowed, his head looked
like a walnut. The thoughts inside were walnut-flavored:
smooth and sweet, but in the end, empty-tasting.

To the old man's right sat Wu Cuiyuan, who looked
like one of those young Christian wives, though she was
still unmarried. Her Chinese gown of white cotton was
trimmed with a narrow blue border—the navy blue around
the white reminded one of the black borders around an
obituary—and she carried a little blue-and-white checked
parasol. Her hairstyle was utterly banal, so as not to attract
attention. Actually, she hadn't much reason to fear. She
wasn't bad-looking, but hers was an uncertain, unfocused
beauty, an afraid-she-had-offended-someone kind of
beauty. Her face was bland, slack, lacking definition. Even
her own mother couldn't say for certain whether her face
was long or round.

At home she was a good daughter, at school she was
a good student. After graduating from college, Cuiyuan
had become an English instructor at her alma mater. Now,
stuck in the air raid, she decided to grade a few papers

while she waited. The first one was written by a male student. It railed against the evils of the big city, full of righteous anger, the prose stiff, choppy, ungrammatical. "Painted prostitutes . . . cruising the Cosmo . . . low-class bars and dancing halls." Cuiyuan paused for a moment, then pulled out her red pencil and gave the paper an "A." Ordinarily, she would have gone right on to the next one, but now, because she had too much time to think, she couldn't help wondering why she had given this student such a high mark. If she hadn't asked herself this question, she could have ignored the whole matter, but once she did ask, her face suffused with red. Suddenly, she understood: it was because this student was the only man who fearlessly and forthrightly said such things to her.

He treated her like an intelligent, sophisticated person; as if she were a man, someone who really understood. He respected her. Cuiyuan always felt that no one at school respected her—from the president on down to the professors, the students, even the janitors. The students' grumbling was especially hard to take: "This place is really falling apart. Getting worse every day. It's bad enough having to learn English from a Chinese, but then to learn it from a Chinese who's never gone abroad . . ." Cuiyuan took abuse at school, took abuse at home. The Wu household was a modern, model household, devout and serious. The family had pushed their daughter to study hard, to climb upward step by step, right to the tip-top. . . . A girl in her twenties teaching at a university! It set a record for women's professional achievement. But her parents' enthusiasm began to wear thin and now they wished she hadn't been quite so serious, wished she'd taken more time out from her studies, tried to find herself a rich husband.

She was a good daughter, a good student. All the people in her family were good people; they took baths every day and read the newspaper; when they listened to the wireless, they never tuned in to local folk-opera, comic opera, that sort of thing, but listened only to the symphonies of Beethoven and Wagner; they didn't understand what they were listening to, but still they listened. In this world, there are more good people than real people. . . . Cuiyuan wasn't very happy.

Life was like the Bible, translated from Hebrew into Greek, from Greek into Latin, from Latin into English, from English into Chinese. When Cuiyuan read it, she translated the standard Chinese into Shanghainese. Gaps were unavoidable.

She put the student's essay down and buried her chin in her hands. The sun burned down on her backbone.

Next to her sat a nanny with a small child lying on her lap. The sole of the child's foot pushed against Cuiyuan's leg. Little red shoes, decorated with tigers, on a soft but tough little foot . . . this at least was real.

A medical student who was also on the tram took out a sketchpad and carefully added the last touches to a diagram of the human skeleton. The other passengers thought he was sketching a portrait of the man who sat dozing across from him. Nothing else was going on, so they started sauntering over, crowding into little clumps of three or four, leaning on each other with their hands behind their backs, gathering around to watch the man sketch from life. The husband who dangled smoked fish from his fingers whispered to his wife: "I can't get used to this cubism, this impressionism, which is so popular these days." "Your pants," she hissed.

The medical student meticulously wrote in the names of every bone, muscle, nerve, and tendon. An office worker hid half his face behind a fan and quietly informed his colleague: "The influence of Chinese painting. Nowadays, writing words in is all the rage in Western painting. Clearly a case of 'Eastern ways spreading Westward.'"

Lu Zongzhen didn't join the crowd, but stayed in his seat. He had decided he was hungry. With everyone gone, he could comfortably munch his spinach-stuffed dumplings. But then he looked up and caught a glimpse, in the third-class car, of a relative, his wife's cousin's son. He detested that Dong Peizhi was a man of humble origins who harbored a great ambition: he sought a fiancée of comfortable means, to serve as a foothold for his climb upward. Lu Zongzhen's eldest daughter had just turned twelve, but already she had caught Peizhi's eye; having made, in his own mind, a pleasing calculation, Peizhi's manner grew ever softer, ever more cunning.

As soon as Lu Zongzhen caught sight of this young man, he was filled with quiet alarm, fearing that if he were seen, Peizhi would take advantage of the opportunity to press forward with his attack. The idea of being stuck in the same car with Dong Peizhi while the city was sealed off was too horrible to contemplate! Lu quickly closed his briefcase and wrapped up his dumplings, then fled, in a great rush, to a seat across the aisle. Now, thank God, he was screened by Wu Cuiyuan, who occupied the seat next to him, and his nephew could not possibly see him.

Cuiyuan turned and gave him a quick look. Oh no! The woman surely thought he was up to no good, changing seats for no reason like that. He recognized the look of a woman being flirted with—she held her face absolutely motionless, no hint of a smile anywhere in her eyes, her mouth, not even in the little hollows beside her nose; yet from some unknown place there was the trembling of a little smile that could break out at any moment. If you think you're simply too adorable, you can't keep from smiling.

Damn! Dong Peizhi had seen him after all and was coming toward the first-class car, very humble, bowing even at a distance, with his long jowls, shiny red cheeks, and long, gray, monklike gown—a clean, cautious young man, hardworking no matter what the hardship, the very epitome of a good son-in-law. Thinking fast, Zongzhen decided to follow Peizhi's lead and try a bit of artful nonchalance. So he stretched one arm out across the windowsill that ran behind Cuiyuan, soundlessly announcing flirtatious intent. This would not, he knew, scare Peizhi into immediate retreat, because in Peizhi's eyes he already was a dirty old man. The way Peizhi saw it, anyone over thirty was old, and all the old were vile. Having seen his uncle's disgraceful behavior, the young man would feel compelled to tell his wife every little detail—well, angering his wife was just fine with him. Who told her to give him such a nephew, anyway? If she was angry, it served her right.

He didn't care much for this woman sitting next to him. Her arms were fair, all right, but were like squeezed-out toothpaste. Her whole body was like squeezed-out toothpaste, it had no shape.

"When will this air raid ever end?" he said in a low, smiling voice. "It's awful!"

Shocked, Cuiyuan turned her head, only to see that his arm was stretched out behind her. She froze. But come what may, Zongzhen could not let himself pull his arm back. His nephew stood just across the way, watching him with brilliant, glowing eyes, the hint of an understanding smile on his face. If, in the middle of everything, he turned and looked his nephew in the eye, maybe the little no-account would get scared, would lower his eyes, flustered and embarrassed like a sweet young thing; then again, maybe Peizhi would keep staring at him—who could tell?

He gritted his teeth and renewed the attack. "Aren't you bored? We could talk a bit, that can't hurt. Let's . . . let's talk," He couldn't control himself, his voice was plaintive.

Again Cuiyuan was shocked. She turned to look at him. Now he remembered, he had seen her get on the tram—a striking image, but an image concocted by chance, not by any intention of hers. "You know, I saw you get on the train," he said softly. "Near the front of the car. There's a torn advertisement, and I saw your profile, just a bit of your chin, through the torn spot." It was an ad for Lacova powdered milk that showed a pudgy little child. Beneath the child's ear this woman's chin had suddenly appeared; it was a little spooky, when you thought about it. "Then you looked down to get some change out of your purse, and I saw your eyes, then your brows, then your hair." When you took her features separately, looked at them one by one, you had to admit she had a certain charm.

Cuiyuan smiled. You wouldn't guess that this man could talk so sweetly—you'd think he was the stereotypical respectable businessman. She looked at him again. Under the tip of his nose the cartilage was reddened by the sunlight. Stretching out from his sleeve, and resting on the newspaper, was a warm, tanned hand, one with feeling—a real person! Not too honest, not too bright, but a real person. Suddenly she felt flushed and happy; she turned away with a murmur. "Don't talk like that."

"What?" Zongzhen had already forgotten what he'd said. His eyes were fixed on his nephew's back—the diplomatic young man had decided that three's a crowd, and he didn't want to offend his uncle. They would meet again, anyway, since theirs was a close family, and no knife was sharp enough to sever the ties; and so he returned to the third-class car. Once Peizhi was gone, Zongzhen withdrew his arm; his manner turned respectable. Casting about for a way to make conversation, he glanced at the notebook spread out on her lap. "Shenguang University," he read aloud. "Are you a student there?"

Did he think she was that young? That she was still a student? She laughed, without answering.

"I graduated from Huaqi." He repeated the name. "Huaqi." On her neck was a tiny dark mole, like the imprint of a fingernail. Zongzhen absentmindedly rubbed the fingers of his right hand across the nails of his left. He coughed slightly, then continued: "What department are you in?" Cuiyuan saw that he had moved his arm and thought that her standoffish manner had wrought this change. She therefore felt she could not refuse to answer. "Literature. And you?"

"Business." Suddenly he felt that their conversation had grown stuffy. "In school I was busy with student activities. Now that I'm out, I'm busy earning a living. So I've never really studied much of anything."

"Is your office very busy?"

"Terribly. In the morning I go to work and in the evening I go home, but I don't know why I do either. I'm not the least bit interested in my job. Sure, it's a way to earn money, but I don't know who I'm earning it for."

"Everyone has family to think of."

"Oh, you don't know . . . my family." A short cough. "We'd better not talk about it"

"Here it comes," thought Cuiyuan. "His wife doesn't understand him. Every married man in the world seems desperately in need of another woman's understanding."

Zongzhen hesitated, then swallowed hard and forced the words out: "My wife—she doesn't understand me at all."

Cuiyuan knitted her brow and looked at him, expressing complete sympathy.

"I really don't understand why I go home every evening. Where is there to go? I have no home, in fact." He removed his glasses, held them up to the light, and wiped the spots off with a handkerchief. Another little cough.

"Just keep going, keep getting by, without thinking—above all, don't start thinking!" Cuiyuan always felt that when nearsighted people took their glasses off in front of other people it was a little obscene; improper, somehow, like taking your clothes off in public. Zongzhen continued: "You, you don't know what kind of woman she is."

"Then why did you . . . in the first place?"

"Even then I was against it. My mother arranged the marriage. Of course I wanted to choose for myself, but . . . she used to be very beautiful . . . I was very young . . . young people, you know. . . ." Cuiyuan nodded her head. "Then she changed into this kind of person—even my mother fights with her, and she blames me for having married her! She has such a temper—she hasn't even got a grade-school education."

Cuiyuan couldn't help saying, with a tiny smile, "You seem to take diplomas very seriously. Actually, even if a woman's educated it's all the same." She didn't know why she said this, wounding her own heart

"Of course, you can laugh, because you're well-educated. You don't know what kind of—" He stopped, breathing hard, and took off the glasses he had just put back on.

"Getting a little carried away?" said Cuiyuan.

Zongzhen gripped his glasses tightly, made a painful gesture with his hands. "You don't know what kind of—"

"I know, I know," Cuiyuan said hurriedly, She knew that if he and his wife didn't get along, the fault could not lie entirely with her. He too was a person of simple intellect. He just wanted a woman who would comfort and forgive him.

The street erupted in noise, as two trucks full of soldiers rumbled by. Cuiyuan and Zongzhen stuck their heads out to see what was going on; to their surprise, their faces came very close together. At close range anyone's face is somehow different, is tension-charged like a close-up on the movie screen. Zongzhen and Cuiyuan suddenly felt they were seeing each other for the first time. To his eyes, her face was the spare, simple peony of a watercolor sketch, and the strands of hair fluttering at her temples were pistils ruffled by a breeze.

He looked at her, and she blushed, When she let him see her blush, he grew visibly happy. Then she blushed even more deeply.

Zongzhen had never thought he could make a woman blush, make her smile, make her hang her head shyly. In this he was a man. Ordinarily, he was an accountant, a father, the head of a household, a tram passenger, a store customer, an insignificant citizen of a big city. But to this woman, this woman who didn't know anything about his life, he was only and entirely a man.

They were in love. He told her all kinds of things: who was on his side at the bank and who secretly opposed him; how his family squabbled; his secret sorrows; his schoolboy dreams . . . unending talk, but she was not put off. Men in love have always liked to talk; women in love, on the other hand, don't want to talk, because they know, without even knowing that they know, that once a man really understands a woman he'll stop loving her.

Zongzhen was sure that Cuiyuan was a lovely woman— pale, wispy, warm, like the breath your mouth exhales in winter. You don't want her, and she quietly drifts away. Being part of you, she understands everything, forgives everything, You tell the truth, and her heart aches for you; you tell a lie, and she smiles as if to say, "Go on with you—what are you saying?"

Zongzhen was quiet for a moment, then said, "I'm thinking of marrying again."

Cuiyuan assumed an air of shocked surprise. "You want a divorce? Well . . . that isn't possible, is it?"

"I can't get a divorce. I have to think of the children's well-being. My oldest daughter is twelve, just passed the entrance exams for middle school, her grades are quite good."

"What," thought Cuiyuan, "what does this have to do with what you just said?" "Oh," she said aloud, her voice cold, "you plan to take a concubine."

"I plan to treat her like a wife," said Zongzhen. "I—I can make things nice for her. I wouldn't do anything to upset her."

"But," said Cuiyuan, "a girl from a good family won't agree to that, will she? So many legal difficulties . . ."

Zongzhen sighed. "Yes, you're right. I can't do it. Shouldn't have mentioned it . . . I'm too old. Thirty-four already."

"Actually," Cuiyuan spoke very slowly, "these days, that isn't considered very old."

Zongzhen was still. Finally he asked, "How old are you?"

Cuiyuan ducked her head. "Twenty-four."

Zongzhen waited awhile, then asked, "Are you a free woman?"

Cuiyuan didn't answer. "You aren't free," said Zongzhen. "But even if you agreed, your family wouldn't, right?"

Cuiyuan pursed her lips. Her family—her prim and proper family—how she hated them all. They had cheated her long enough. They wanted her to find them a wealthy son-in-law. Well, Zongzhen didn't have money, but he did have a wife—that would make them good and angry! It would serve them right!

Little by little, people started getting back on the tram. Perhaps it was rumored out there that "traffic will soon return to normal." The passengers got on and sat down, pressing against Zongzhen and Cuiyuan, forcing them a little closer, then a little closer again.

Zongzhen and Cuiyuan wondered how they could have been so foolish not to have thought of sitting closer before. Zongzhen struggled against his happiness. He turned to her and said, in a voice full of pain, "No, this won't do! I can't let you sacrifice your future! You're a fine person, with such a good education . . . I don't have much money, and don't want to ruin your life!"

Well, of course, it was money again. What he said was true. "It's over," thought Cuiyuan. In the end she'd probably marry, but her husband would never be as dear as this stranger met by chance—this man on the tram in the middle of a sealed-off city . . . it could never be this spontaneous again. Never again . . . oh, this man, he was so stupid! So very stupid! All she wanted was one small part of him, one little part that no one else could want. He was throwing away his own happiness. Such an idiotic waste! She wept, but it wasn't a gentle, maidenly weeping. She practically spit her tears into his face. He was a good person—the world had gained one more good person! What use would it be to explain this to him? If a woman needs to turn to words to move a man's heart, she is a sad case. Once Zongzhen got anxious, he couldn't get any words out, and just kept shaking the umbrella she was holding. She ignored him. Then he tugged at her hand. "Hey, there are people here, you know! Don't! Don't get so upset! Wait a bit, and we'll talk it over on the telephone. Give me your number." Cuiyuan didn't answer. He pressed her. "You have to give me your phone number."

"Seven-five-three-six-nine." Cuiyuan spoke as fast as she could.

"Seven-five-three-six-nine?"

No response. "Seven-five-three-six-nine, seven-five . . ." Mumbling the number over and over, Zongzhen searched his pockets for a pen, but the more frantic he became, the harder it was to find one. Cuiyuan had a red pencil in her bag, but she purposely did not take it out. He ought to remember her telephone number; if he didn't, then he didn't love her, and there was no point in continuing the conversation.

The city started up again. Ding-ding-ding-ding. Every "ding" a cold little dot, which added up to a line that cut across time and space.

A wave of cheers swept across the metropolis. The tram started clanking its way forward. Zongzhen stood up, pushed into the crowd, and disappeared; Cuiyuan turned her head away, as if she didn't care. He was gone. To her, it was as if he were dead.

The tram picked up speed. On the evening street, a tofu-seller had set his shoulder-pole down and was holding up a rattle; eyes shut, he shook it back and forth. A big-boned blonde woman, straw hat slung across her back, bantered with an Italian sailor. All her teeth showed when she grinned. When Cuiyuan looked at these people, they lived for that one moment. Then the tram clanked onward, and one by one they died away.

Cuiyuan shut her eyes fretfully. If he phoned her, she wouldn't be able to control her voice; it would be filled with emotion, for he was a man who had died, then returned to life.

The lights inside the tram went on; she opened her eyes and saw him sitting in his old seat, looking remote. She trembled with shock—he hadn't gotten off the tram, after all! Then she understood his meaning: everything that had happened while the city was sealed was a non-occurrence. The whole of Shanghai had dozed off, had dreamed an unreasonable dream.

The tramcar driver raised his voice in song: "Sad, sad, sad! No money do I have! Sad, sad, sad—" An old beggar, thoroughly dazed, limped across the street in front of the tram. The driver bellowed at her. "You swine!"

Translated by Karen Kingsbury

The Longtang

Wang Anyi

FOR SOMEONE LOOKING down from the highest point in the city, Shanghai's *longtang*—her vast neighborhoods inside enclosed alleys—are a magnificent sight. The longtang are the backdrop of this city. Streetlights and buildings rise around them in a series of dots and lines, like the subtle brush strokes that bring life to the empty expanses of white paper in a traditional Chinese landscape painting. As day turns into night and the city lights up, these dots and lines begin to glimmer. However, underneath the glitter lies an immense blanket of darkness—these are the longtang of Shanghai.

WANG ANYI (1954–) appeared on the literary scene in the aftermath of the Cultural Revolution. Her writing ranges from intimate stories about men and women to "nativist" fiction set in the countryside. In recent years, her fiction has focused on Shanghai. This excerpt is from her most famous novel, *Song of Everlasting Sorrow* (1995), which chronicles the life of Wang Qiyao, daughter of a middle-class Shanghai family, from the 1940s to the 1980s. As this piece suggests, the city of Shanghai itself plays a central role in the novel. It describes in loving detail the *longtang*, the alleyways where Shanghai's emerging middle class resided in the 1930s and 1940s.

The darkness looks almost to be a series of furious waves that threaten to wash away the glowing dots and lines. It has volume, whereas all those lines and dots float on the surface—they are there only to differentiate the areas of this dark mass, like punctuation marks whose job it is to break up an essay into sentences and paragraphs. The darkness is like an abyss—even a mountain falling in would be swallowed whole and sink silently to the bottom. Countless reefs lurk beneath this swelling ocean of darkness, where one false move could capsize a ship. The darkness buoys up Shanghai's handful of illuminated lines and dots, supporting them decade after decade. Against this decades-old backdrop of darkness, the Paris of the Orient unfolds her splendor.

Today, everything looks worn out, exposing bit by bit what lies underneath. One strand at a time, the first rays of the morning sun shine through just as, one by one, the city lights go out. Everything begins from a cover of light fog, through which a horizontal ray of light crafts an outline as if drawing it out with a fine brush. First to appear are the dormer windows protruding from the rooftop garrets of those traditional longtang buildings, showing themselves off with a certain self-conscious delicacy; the wooden shutters are carefully delineated, the handmade rooftop tiles are arranged with precision, even the potted roses on the windowsills have been cared for painstakingly.

Next to emerge are the balconies; here articles of clothing hung out to dry the night before cling motionless like a scene out of a painting. The cement on the balustrade peels away to reveal the rusty red bricks beneath—this too looks as if painted in a picture, each brushstroke appearing clear and distinct. After that come the cracked gable walls, lined with traces of green moss that look cold and clammy to the touch. The first rays of light shining on the gable walls create a stunning picture, a gorgeous portrait, bearing just a hint of desolation, fresh and new yet not without a past.

At this moment the cement pavement of the longtang is still enveloped in fog, which lingers thick in the back alleys. But on the iron-railed balconies of the newer long-tang apartments the sunlight is already striking the glass panes on the French doors, which refract the light. This stroke is a relatively sharp one, and seems to pull back the curtain that separates day from night. The sunlight finally drives away the fog, washing everything in its path with a palette of strong color. The moss turns out to be not green but a dark raven hue, the wooden window frames start to blacken, and the iron railing on the balcony becomes a rusted yellow. One can see blades of green grass grow-ing from between the cracks in the gables, and the white pigeons turn gray as they soar up into the sky.

Shanghai's longtang come in many different forms, each with colors and sounds of its own. Unable to decide on any one appearance, they remain fickle, sometimes looking like this, sometimes looking like that. Actually, despite their constant fluctuations, they always remain the same—the shape may shift but the spirit is unchanged. Back and forth they go, but in the end it's the same old story, like an army of a thousand united by a single goal.

Those longtang that have entryways with stone gates emanate an aura of power. They have inherited the style of Shanghai's glorious old mansions. Sporting the facade of an official residence, they make it a point to have a grandiose entrance and high surrounding walls. But, upon entering, one discovers that the courtyard is modest and the reception area narrow—two or three steps and you are already at the wooden staircase across the room. The staircase is not curved, but leads straight up into the bedroom, where a window overlooking the street hints at romantic ardor.

The trendy longtang neighborhoods in the eastern district of Shanghai have done away with such haughty airs. They greet you with low wrought-iron gates of floral design. For them a small window overlooking a side street is not enough; they all have to have walk-out balconies, the better to enjoy the street scenery. Fragrant oleanders reach out over the courtyard walls, as if no longer able to contain their springtime passion. Deep down, however, those inside still have their guard up: the back doors are bolted shut with spring locks of German manufacture, the windows on the ground floor all have steel bars, the low front gates of wrought iron are crowned with ornamented spikes, and walls protect the courtyard on all sides. One may enter at will, but escape seems virtually impossible.

On the western side of the city, the apartment-style longtang take an even stricter approach to security. These structures are built in clusters, with doors that look as if not even an army of ten thousand could force their way inside. The walls are soundproof so that people living even in close quarters cannot hear one another, and the buildings are widely spaced so that neighbors can avoid one another. This is security of a democratic sort—trans-Atlantic style—to ensure and protect individual freedom. Here people can do whatever their hearts desire, and there is no one to stop them.

The longtang in the slums are open-air. The makeshift roofs leak in the rain, the thin plywood walls fail to keep out the wind, and the doors and windows never seem to close properly. Apartment structures are built virtually on top of one another, cheek by jowl, breathing down upon each other's necks. Their lights are like tiny glowing peas, not very bright, but dense as a pot of pea porridge. Like a great river, these longtang have innumerable tributaries, and their countless branches resemble those of a tall tree. Criss-crossing, they form a giant web. On the surface they appear entirely exposed, but in reality they conceal a complex inner soul that remains mysterious, unfathomable.

As dusk approaches, flocks of pigeons hover about the Shanghai skyline in search of their nests. The rooftop ridges rise and fall, extending into the distance; viewed from the side, they form an endless mountain range, and from the front, a series of vertical summits. Viewed from the highest peak, they merge into one boundless vista that looks the same from all directions. Like water flowing aimlessly, they seem to creep into every crevice and crack, but upon closer inspection they fall into an orderly pattern. At once dense and wide-ranging, they resemble rye fields where the farmers, having scattered their seeds, are now harvesting a rich crop. Then again, they are a little like a pristine forest, living and dying according to its own cycle. Altogether they make for a scene of the utmost beauty and splendor.

The longtang of Shanghai exude a sensuality like the intimacy of flesh on flesh—cool and warm, tangible and knowable, a little self-centered. The grease-stained rear kitchen window is where the *amah* gossips. Beside the window is the back door; from this the eldest daughter goes out to school and holds her secret rendezvous with her boyfriend. The front door, reserved for distinguished guests, opens only on important occasions. On each side of the door hang couplets announcing marriages, funerals, and other family events. The door seems always to be in a state of uncontrollable, even garrulous, excitement. Echoes of secret whispers linger around the flat roof, the balcony, and the windows. At night, the sounds of rapping on the doors rise and fall in the darkness.

To return to the highest point in the city and look down on it from another angle: clothes hanging out to dry on the cluttered bamboo poles hint at the private lives and loves that lie hidden beneath. In the garden, potted balsams, gem flowers, scallions, and garlic also breathe the faint air of a secret affair. The empty pigeon cage up on the roof is an empty heart. Broken roof tiles lying in disarray are symbols of the body and soul. Some of the gully-like alleys are lined with cement, others with cobblestone. The cement alleys make you feel cut off, while the cobblestone alleys give the sensation of a fleshy hand. Footsteps sound different in these two types of longtang. The former is crisp and bright, but the latter is something that you absorb and keep inside. The former is a collection of polite pleasantries, the latter of words spoken from the bottom of one's heart. Neither is like an official document; both belong to the necessary language of the everyday.

The back alleys of Shanghai try even harder to work their way into people's hearts. The pavement is covered with a layer of cracks. Gutters overflow; floating in the discolored water are fish scales and rotten vegetable leaves, as well as the greasy lampblack from the stovetop. It is dirty and grimy, impure, here. Here the most private secrets are exposed, and not always in the most conventional fashion. Because of this a pall hangs over these back alleys. The sunlight does not shine through until three o'clock in the afternoon, and before long the sun begins to set in the west. But this little bit of sunlight envelops the back alleys in a blanket of warm color. The walls turn a brilliant yellow, highlighting the unevenness of the rough whetstone and giving it the texture of coarse sand. The windows also turn a golden yellow, but they are scratched and stained. By now the sun has been shining down for a long time and is beginning to show signs of fatigue. Summoning up the last vestiges of radiance from the depths, the lingering rays of sunlight flicker with a sticky thickness of built-up residue, rather dirty. As twilight encroaches, flocks of pigeons soar overhead, dust motes drift, and stray cats wander in and out of sight. This is a feeling that, having penetrated the flesh, goes beyond closeness. One begins to weary of it. It breeds a secret fear, but hidden within that fear is an excitement that gnaws down to the bone.

What moves you about the longtang of Shanghai stems from the most mundane scenes: not the surging rush of clouds and rain, but something steadily accumulated over time. It is the excitement of cooking smoke and human vitality. Something is flowing through the longtang that is unpredictable yet entirely rational, small, not large, and trivial—but then even a castle can be made out of sand. It has nothing to do with things like "history," not even "unofficial history": we can only call it gossip.

Gossip is yet another landscape in the Shanghai longtang—you can almost see it as it sneaks out through the rear windows and the back doors. What emerges from the front doors and balconies is a bit more proper—but it is still gossip. These rumors may not necessarily qualify as history, but they carry with them the shadows of time. There is order in their progression, which follows the law of preordained consequences. These rumors cling to the skin and stick to the flesh; they are not cold or stiff, like a pile of musty old books. Though marred by untruths, these are falsehoods that have feeling.

When the city's streetlights are ablaze, its longtang remain in darkness, save the lonely street lamps hanging on the alley corners. The lamps, enclosed in crude frames of rusty iron covered with dust, emit a murky yellow glow. On the ground, a shroud of thick mist forms and begins to spread out—this is the time when rumors and gossip start to brew. It is a gloomy hour, when nothing is clear, yet it is enough to break the heart. Pigeons coo in their cages, talking their language of secret whispers. The streetlights shine with a prim and proper light, but as soon as that light streams into the longtang alleys, it is overwhelmed by darkness. The kind of gossip exchanged in the front rooms and adjoining wings belongs to the old school and smacks faintly of potpourri. The gossip in the rooftop garrets and staircases is new school and smells of mothballs. But, old school or new, gossip is always told in earnest—you could even say it is told in the spirit of truth.

This is like scooping water with one's hands: even though you might lose half the water along the way, with enough persistence you can still fill up a pond. Or like the swallow that, though she may drop half the earth and twigs she is carrying in her beak, can still build a nest— there is no need for laziness or trickery. The longtang of Shanghai are an unbearable sight. The patches of green moss growing in the shade are, in truth, like scars growing over a wound; it takes time for the wound to heal. It is because the moss lacks a proper place that it grows in the shade and shadows—years go by and it never sees the sun. Now ivy grows out in the open, but it serves as Time's curtain and always has something to hide. The pigeons gaze down at the outstretching billows of roof tiles as they take to the air, and their hearts are stabbed with pain. Coming up over the longtang rooftops, the sun shoots out its belabored rays—a majestic sight pieced together from countless minute fragments, an immense power born of immeasurable patience.

Translated by Michael Berry and Susan Chan Egan

Black Bristle, White Bristles

Yan Lianke

SPRING OUGHT TO FEEL LIKE SPRING, with flowers and grass, light blues and gentle breezes. Or else lush greens, fragrances that assault your nostrils like the aroma of bottled spirits emerging from far down a lane. But at dusk the residents of Wu Family Slope detected the rank odor of blood, dripping red, coming on the air from the ridge line, dark purple splotches of it, like a verdant spring grove dotted with autumn persimmons. What's that smell? someone asked. People who had taken their dinner

---

YAN LIANKE (1958–) has been writing since the 1980s, but it was not until 2000 that he started gaining a national reputation. His novels have been extremely controversial, subject to censorship and sometimes banned: *Serve the People* (2005), a sex-filled satire of the Cultural Revolution Mao cult; *Pleasure* (2004), an experimental novel about utopia and dystopia; and *Dreams of Ding Village* (2006), a haunting work about an AIDS-ravaged village in Yan's native Henan. Translated especially for this volume, "White Bristle, Black Bristles" (2003) is a biting analysis of the workings of political power in a rural village—a critique of a political system that pushes people to blindly serve power. The village head never appears in the story, but his symbolic presence affects the actions of the main protagonists.

---

over to the dining area at the village entrance stopped eating, their rice bowls frozen in mid-air, and sniffed deeply; they all smelled the blood.

— Pig Butcher Li is slaughtering another pig.

That comment broke the silence and sent people back to eating and drinking. Everyone knew that tomorrow would be the last market day of the third lunar month, and that slaughtering pigs for the market was what the butcher did. But in the past he'd always done his killing before sunrise so he could be on the road by dawn and sell the meat in town while it was still fresh. Why was he doing it at sunset? And why was the smell of blood stronger than before? Those were only fleeting thoughts by the villagers. By then it was mid-spring and the wheat, which had emerged from hibernation, rustled as it grew. Grass too shot up out of the ground. Time to hoe the fields, time to fertilize the crops and irrigate, at least where there was water to be found. Each family was as busy as migrating ants, and had no time to worry about anyone else.

The dining area was located at the head of the village. Butcher Li's family lived on the ridge, near the road, not far from a three-way intersection. Though he had abandoned farming for commerce, proximity to the road was still important: engaged in the business of animal slaughter, he needed the benefits of convenient transportation, since that made it so much easier when he was asked to dispatch animals for weddings and funerals in neighboring villages. That is why the Li family had moved to the ridge from the village— prosperity and convenience. They built a two-story house with a tiled roof girded by a brick wall. The slaughtering was carried out on the ground floor, where the family ran a convenience shop, selling odds and ends, snacks, and some prepared foods. The upstairs living quarters included two rooms that were sometimes made available to paying guests, weary travelers who sought rest for the night. First they'd enjoy simple fare and drink downstairs until they could barely stand, then they'd make their way up to one of the guest rooms for the night. The next morning, sober and rested, they'd settle up and be on their way.

Even though the rooms were austere to the point of squalor, with a simple bed, a table, and a naked fifteen-watt bulb (plus a squat candle for electrical outages), the secretary of the county Party committee had actually spent a night in one of them. Someone said he'd had no choice, that his car had broken down. But, according to Butcher Li, whoever said that was talking through his ass. Tell me this: Would a chauffeur ever let something like that happen to a Party secretary's car? No, he said that Party Secretary Zhao had spent the night to see first-hand how the common folk were prospering and to pass the time chatting with Butcher Li. What cannot be disputed is the fact that Party Secretary Zhao spent a night in the room, and that led to a significant rise in the Li family's fortunes. The table, bed, mattress pad, wash basin, and slippers in the eastern guest room, all mementoes of Secretary Zhao's brief visit, were properly cleaned and put in good order to be used by future occupants at a cost of fifteen yuan, which was a fifty percent increase over the pre-Zhao era. Passersby were not immune to weighing the good against the bad, and despite the inflated cost, the eastern guest room was where they chose to stay; it was, after all, the room where Secretary Zhao had spent a night. Long-distance truckers pressed down on the gas pedal for as long as it took in order to spend the night in the eastern guest room. To be sure, no resident of Wu Family Slope overlooked the added attraction that the Li family also supplied tasty meat and undiluted liquor. Nothing that happened at the Li house by the ridge road ever surprised people, since, after all, Secretary Zhao had spent the night there.

Market day had arrived, and the slaughter that should have occurred in the early morning had been moved ahead to the hours before sunset, sending the stench of blood into the late-night spring air. So what? All he had to do was put the animal to the knife and spread the split halves out on a butcher block, then wash them down with clean water and cover them with a sheet of plastic. After that, who could tell that the meat wasn't fresh?

The people kept eating, and the chatter never stopped. Those with empty rice bowls got up, went home, and refilled them, while those who didn't feel like going sent their children, who grumbled about being asked, since they'd just come from home with their own food. That attitude earned them a scolding from unhappy parents who called them spoiled brats, too lazy to even run home for a bowl of soupy rice. If I'd known how you were going to turn out, I'd never have had you in the first place, a comment that made the children very unhappy, since they'd only stalled a minute or two and hadn't said they wouldn't go; but their parents gave them hell. I never asked to be born, did I? they fired back. What could any parent say to that? Nothing. So they reached down, removed one of the shoes they were sitting on, and flung it at their disobedient offspring, filling the sky above the dining area with dust. Rice bowls were quickly tucked under arms or against chests for protection. As the clamor rose, a voice from outside stilled the crowd: What the hell's going on in there? What's wrong with your folks telling you to go get them something to eat, huh?

The area quieted down immediately. Knowing they'd taken things too far, the chastised children held their tongues, as all eyes turned in the direction of the ridge road. Li Xing, the butcher, had come down from the ridge.

Liu Genbao came home from the dining area looking like a man who'd entered an examination hall after leaving the freedom of broad, open fields—tentative and a little uneasy. Father was out in the yard enjoying an after-dinner smoke, the bowl of his pipe glowing one minute and darkening the next, sending flickers of light into the dark sky. Mother was in the kitchen cleaning up, creating a chorus of clanging cookware that was quickly drowned out by splashing water—crisp, watery sounds. Genbao walked into the kitchen and laid his half-full rice bowl down on top of the stove. There was something he wanted to say, but he just stood there looking at his mother for a moment before turning and walking back outside.

He crouched down in front of Father.

Something on your mind? Father asked.

No, not really.

Whatever it is, go on, say it.

I want to do some prison time.

That stunned his father, whose pipe bowl flared up as he sucked in hard; his face froze, like a bowl of soft noodles suddenly turning to stone. Removing the pipe from his mouth, he glared at his son as he would an inquisitive passerby.

What did you say, Genbao?

Genbao looked into his father's face, but was unable to gauge the depth of the older man's bewilderment or the weight of his concern, all thanks to the absence of light— nothing but a black form, like a mighty tree, standing immovably before him. No sense in gazing any longer, since there was nothing to see. So he took off a shoe and sat down on it opposite his father, resting his arms on his knees and rubbing his hands together, as if shucking peas. He left his father's question hanging in the air.

What did you just say, Genbao? his father repeated.

I want to see what you think, Dad, Genbao said. If you and Mother agree, I want to do prison time for somebody.

Have you lost your damned mind! his father roared.

Genbao's head drooped. I said I want to know what you think, didn't I?

After a tense pause, his father asked, For who?

The town head.

The town head? His father's head jerked up.

Yes.

Are you telling me the town head wants you to go to prison for him? Father said with a smirk.

Back at the dining area I heard Butcher Li say that the town head was driving on the ridge at dusk and ran over a twenty-year-old farmer from Zhang Fort Village. It was his fault, since it was his car, but he is the town head, and who'd be crazy enough to say that to him? So somebody has to go to the traffic office and take the blame. Whoever it is has to say he got drunk at Butcher Li's and accidentally ran the young man down with his tractor. After that, no sweat. The town head will see to everything. There'll have to be a cash settlement with the people of Zhang Fort Village, and he'll take care of that. Then whoever takes the blame for the accident will spend a few weeks in prison.

Finally, the moon made an appearance over Wu Family Slope, which was so quiet it was as if no such place even existed. Except for the shuffling footsteps heading east and moving out of earshot, disappearing at Butcher Li's house. Genbao's mother, who had heard every word of the conversation, said nothing. Instead, she picked up a basket of peanuts, moved a stool over to a spot between her husband and her son, and set the bowl on it. Then she sat down in front of the stool and gazed at her boy and then looked at her husband, sighing heavily as she entered the profound silence between father and son.

Some background on Genbao: he'd reached the age of twenty-nine without managing to attract a wife, which made the Liu family unique in the village. The reason? Poverty alone can't be blamed; no, that wasn't it. Every family in the village had by then built sturdy homes with tiled roofs, all but the Lius, who still lived in a thatched hut. And Genbao was a timid, guileless fellow who didn't even have the heart to hit an ox with his hoe after the animal had eaten his crops, troubled by the thought of how that would affect the animal's owner. Who would want anyone that worthless for a mate? There'd been opportunities in the past, with prospective wives visiting their home. But nothing ever came of it—no flowers, no fruit. Who'd have thought that after all these years he'd be so unmarriageable that even widows and divorcees shunned him? Six months earlier, a kinsman had wanted to introduce him to a widow who was not only ugly, but, at the age of twenty-six, already had two kids. Genbao was not interested. What's the harm in looking? the matchmaker said. So they met, and she wasted no time.

Are you an only child? she asked.

Yes.

How many Liu families in the village.

Just ours.

Anyone in your family a village or township cadre?

He shook his head.

That was all she needed to know. As she jumped down off her stool she said through her teeth, Why'd you make me come all this way to meet you? Didn't the matchmaker tell you my first husband lost an argument over watering the fields and got punched out in the process? He didn't tell you he came home and hanged himself, or that I'm not interested in money or any other kind of wealth, that all I'm looking for is a man who carries the authority of a man, who isn't a bully but won't back down when he's up against one? Her monologue ended, she turned and started out the door. Out in the yard, she looked around and then spun back to glare at Genbao. I sacrificed a day at the market, she said, and came all the way over here to let you look me over and see if a match was possible. If I'd spent the day selling produce at the market I'd have earned seventy or eighty yuan, money you cost me. I won't ask you to cough up that much, but you ought to at least reimburse me to the tune of fifty, don't you think?

What are you saying? Genbao was incredulous.

You cost me a day's work and I want you to come up with fifty yuan.

Keeping his voice low, Genbao said, Don't you have an ounce of shame?

Okay, I admit I'm shameless. So I'll tell you what. Slug me once and I'll be on my way. Either that or give me fifty yuan, one or the other. If you don't, I'll scream that you've been groping me.

Having no choice, Genbao went inside, got fifty yuan, came back outside, and thrust the bill into her hand. Go on, get out, and don't ever come back to Wu Family Slope.

She took the money, looked down at it, and said, Okay, I'll marry you. All you have to do is slap me.

Go, Genbao said. You've got your money, now leave.

Rough me up a little and I'll give away my two kids to marry you.

You're sick, he said. Sick in the head. Go check yourself in to the psycho ward.

The woman threw the fifty-yuan bill to the ground at Genbao's feet and walked off, stopping just long enough to say, Who'd marry a gutless man like you? That'd be asking for a lifetime of misery.

Truth to tell, no one bullied Genbao or anyone else in his family, but the fact that they were loners, with no relatives in the village, kept Genbao a bachelor. Twenty-nine this year, on his way to thirty, close to half a man's life.

Unmarried at that advanced age not only made it difficult for him to hold his head up in the village, it weighed heavily on his parents as well, who felt they'd failed their only son.

Genbao's father smoked the last of the tobacco in his pipe and refilled it, but instead of lighting it, laid it down beside him, picked up a handful of peanuts, and began shucking them. None made it into his mouth as he sat there looking down at his son. Framed by moonlight, Genbao kept his head down as he sat on his shoe, looking like a shapeless bundle of something. His father cast a glance at the hut he'd long wanted to replace with a real building, but had never found the money he needed. If squat and run-down hadn't been enough to make it an eyesore, then the two grassy indentations on the thatched roof, like a pair of open graves in the moonlight, sealed the deal. The window-less kitchen and a cracked water vat in the doorway were thrown into sharp outline by the moon's rays. The pigpen next to the house had a rammed-earth wall, a framed gate, and a stone trough, all of which made it serviceable and hardy. And yet, inexplicably, they'd had no luck raising pigs. No matter how well they fed them, they all died. So they tried raising goats, and they died. Then they converted the pen into one for chickens, which grew big and fat, and yet, and yet, the hens laid eggs at the glacial speed of one every four or five days. Even in the summer, the egg-laying season, none of them ever managed an egg every two days, while other people's birds laid one a day, sometimes two a day or three every two days. That was life in the Liu family, one that Genbao's father had resigned himself to. Bringing his gaze back to the scene in front of him, he ate the peanuts in his hand and complained that the oil had dried up. They had no taste. Eat them anyway, his wife said. Genbao's uncle dropped them off when he came by the other day. So Genbao's father picked up another handful and shucked them noisily. Here, Genbao, have some.

I don't want any, Genbao said.

How do you know you'll only have to spend a few weeks in prison if you take the blame?

Butcher Li said so.

Who told him?

If anybody knows, it's him. The accident happened right in front of his house, where the Party Secretary once spent the night.

What happens after whoever it is gets out of prison? his mother asked.

Be quiet, woman! So, Genbao, what happens after whoever it is gets out of prison? He can do whatever he wants. He's the town head and he can ask my son to do his prison time.

But then his father turned and gave his son a long look. Go ahead, if that's what you want, go talk to Butcher Li and tell him you're willing to do the man's prison time. But remember, his name is Li Xing, so call him Uncle Li Xing, never call him Butcher Li to his face.

By that time the moon was directly overhead, flooding the yard with light and turning the diaphanous wings of the chirping crickets silvery. Genbao stood up and headed out the gate, followed by his mother, who'd scooped up a handful of peanuts. Here, take these, she said. There's still enough oil in them to keep their taste.

Genbao pushed his mother's hand away. I don't want them, he said as he passed through the gate, and, as if he was off on a long journey, did not look back. He did, however, hear peanuts being shucked behind him. It sounded like someone doing laundry in the moonlight, a crisp, splashing noise that had the intimate effect of making him want to linger awhile.

Things were hopping at Butcher Li's house, illuminated by a pair of 200-watt bulbs that overwhelmed the bright moonbeams. A miner from somewhere had decided to celebrate something or other, making it necessary for Butcher Li to stay up all night slaughtering animals, especially since tomorrow was market day and he had his regular customers to think about. The one block was insufficient for the work ahead, so he took down a door to use as a second one. While the actual slaughtering fell to him, he'd brought in a pair of youngsters from an outside village to help out, for which they were paid ten yuan for every pig that was dispatched.

The compound was alive with people: miners, curious children, and men from neighboring villages who'd brought in pigs and were waiting to put them on the scale. As Genbao left the village he heard blood-curdling squeals emerge from the blocks and he shivered, as if hit by a blast of cold air; but he quickly brought himself under control and stopped shivering. After all, it was pigs being killed, not people. As he walked into Butcher Li's yard through a double gate that could accommodate a truck, the two sides of a de-gutted pig were already hanging by hooks under a canopy, and Butcher Li, stripped to the waist, was washing them down with gourdfuls of clean water, sending rivulets of bloody water onto a concrete slab and into a ditch that ran to the back of the house. The whole world seemed to reek of fresh blood. One of Li's helpers was boiling a vat of water in the corner of the yard to soften the bristles, the other was removing bristles with a metal scraper, producing the eerie stench of a wild animal's burned hide. That stench hung over Butcher Li's yard all year long, and Genbao wondered how the Party secretary could have put up with it for a whole night. But he had. An immaculate sign hung from the eastern second-story guest room on the south side of the building, proclaiming: County Party Secretary Zhao Slept Here. There was enough light for Genbao to see a new sign, this one hanging over the doorway leading to the western guest room; it proclaimed: County Chief Ma Slept Here. Now when had *he* spent the night here? Genbao had to wonder. But he must have done, since that's what the sign said.

With his eyes still on the signs overhead, Genbao made his way through the crowd up to Butcher Li, whose back was to him. Then he waited until the first side of the pig was washed clean before saying tentatively, Uncle Li.

Without responding, Butcher Li brushed drops of bloody water off his shoulders, wiped his sweaty forehead with his forearm, and then stepped up to the blood-streaked second side, where he recommenced scooping out gourdfuls of water. He'd heard the greeting behind him. Is that you, Genbao? he asked as he continued working.

Yes, Uncle Li, it's me.

Butcher Li flung a gourdful of water into the abdomen cavity.

Interested in standing in for the town head, are you? Quite an opportunity. You couldn't pray for a better one.

Genbao took a step backward as bloody water splashed into face.

I talked it over with my dad. I'll do it.

Butcher Li emptied another gourdful of water.

It's not that easy. Go wait inside.

Three people were seated in the ground-floor dining room when Genbao walked in. One of them, Wu Zhuzi, was a forty-year-old man from the west end of the village whose wife had walked out on him, taking their child and moving in with the younger brother of a cadre in another village; nothing could make her come back home, so he was all alone. Next to him was Lame Zhao, from the south end. Things had been going fine for him until he was crippled when a brick kiln collapsed on him. His life collapsed along with it, since he was deeply in debt to the credit cooperative. A villager by the name of Li Qing, the third man, ran a business in town and traveled back and forth in his own Russian automobile. Genbao knew that Zhuzi and the lame villager, like him, were eager to do prison time for the town head, one to get the man's help in coaxing his wife to come back home, the other to help out with his debt to the credit cooperative. Exactly what Li Qing wanted as he sat there at the dining table with the others was a mystery. But three pairs of eyes were fixed on Genbao as he walked in and looked straight at Li Qing, who was a year younger than he.

Like a sneak thief, Li Qing kept his head down. He told them he was hoping the town head could help his younger brother, a recent normal school graduate, find a teaching job in town.

You've already got plenty going for you, Zhuzi said with a sneer, but you want even more.

As Li Qing dropped his head even lower, his face turned as red as the blood on the ground outside.

Why don't you leave, Lame Zhao said to Li Qing with a squint, and let Genbao and us compete for this opportunity, since the three of us are in the same boat?

Li Qing stayed put and smiled sheepishly.

Genbao sat down in an empty chair around the square table, one of those that used to be called "eight immortals" tables, but now, in a nod to city folk, was just an ordinary dining table. A variety of objects, including rice, dry noodles, and cooking oil, occupied most of the thirty or forty square feet in the so-called dining room, and the table took up what little empty space was left. Since they weren't paying customers, no one came to pour tea from the aluminum teapot on the table. Flies and moths circled the light bulb above the table; some of the moths didn't flinch from resting on the bulb itself when they were tired from their dancing, while the flies settled on the men's bodies or the greasy tabletop to catch their breath.

More squeals erupted out in the yard, frighteningly shrill, like train whistles from the other side of the mountain, but shorter and not as rhythmic. Embedded in the sounds were the gasps of a pig and frenzied human shouts. That lasted for only a few moments before silence returned. All four men knew that a knife had been buried in a pig's neck and ripped down into its guts. They next heard Butcher Li tell one helper to take the pig away and scald it, and the other to disembowel a second pig. A discussion over the relative weights of the two pigs followed. The room was warming up. Butcher Li was too busy making a living to walk in, point to one of the men, and say, You can do the prison time for the town head. You other three can go home. Who knows, maybe he wasn't sure who he should pick for this fine opportunity, so he concentrated on slaughtering pigs, not giving a thought to the presence of Genbao, Zhuzi, Lame Zhao, and Li Qing. His wife and children were upstairs watching TV, the sounds of a martial arts film raining down on the visitors like bricks or roof tiles. Genbao looked up at the ceiling; so did the other three men.

It's getting late, Li Qing said.

You can leave if you're tired of waiting, Zhuzi said.

Not me. I'll wait till sunup if I have to.

Lame Zhao looked first at Li Qing and then spun around to stare at Genbao. My friend, he said, you're not like the rest of us. You've never married and you've had an education. Doing time for the town head would ruin your reputation, and you'd never find a wife.

Genbao knew he should respond, but didn't know what to say. So Li Qing spoke up for him. That's where you're wrong. It's exactly what *would* get him a wife. Genbao sent Li Qing a look of gratitude. Li Qing nodded. As a relative of Butcher Li, he felt more comfortable in the house than the others, so he let his eyes roam freely and even went upstairs to watch TV for a while. When he came back down, he walked outside to press Uncle Li to make up his mind who'd be going to prison the next day. But a moment later he came back inside and said, Uncle Li's a busy man. He wants us to choose. Us to choose? Choose who? No way! That'd never work. Glances passed back and forth among them. Since no one was backing out, they all looked away.

The hours passed with the slow clip-clop of a water buffalo, as the night deepened—a bottomless dry well of time for four men. By the time the TV upstairs was turned off, Butcher Li had dispatched five pigs. Zhuzi and Lame Zhao were asleep at the table, heads resting on their arms, and Genbao was sure that Butcher Li had forgotten all about them. But just as he was about to get up and ask Butcher Li who he was going to choose to do the prison time—if it was him, fine; if not, then he'd go home disappointed and get some sleep—there was a banging at the door.

Awake and alert, they all fixed their eyes on the door.

It wasn't Butcher Li. One of his helpers had rapped on the door with the butt of a butcher knife, the impact sending drops of fresh blood falling at his feet, like soft tofu. Seeing they were all awake, he tossed four crumpled pieces of paper onto the table. Butcher Li says it's getting late and there's no need for you all to wait around. There's a black pig bristle in one of those paper lots. The other three have white bristles. Whoever gets the black bristle will be the town head's benefactor. The ones with white bristles won't be. Having said his piece, he stood in the light and looked down at the four paper lots, then at the four men.

They were wide awake now. So, the life-changing opportunity to be the town head's benefactor now hinged on what was in those paper lots, a brightly colored, some-what joyous and auspicious cigarette paper torn into four pieces and crumpled up to contain pig bristles, three of which were white. As they gazed down at the lots lying in front of them, their eyes brightened and grew big; but no one dared pick up the fateful first piece.

Go ahead, the youngster said, pick one, then you can get some sleep. I spent half the night trying to get Butcher Li to let me do the time, but as an outsider, I don't even get a chance to try my luck.

Are you mocking us? Li Qing demanded.

Maybe a little, he replied. I'm young enough to be one of your children. I mean, I've wanted to go into town and rent some rooms from the government to open a shop, but that kind of luck never filters down to peasants like me. Spending a few weeks in prison for the town head would open up all sorts of possibilities for me. I wouldn't have to run around like someone fleeing from the tax man, would I? Now go ahead, make your choices. When you've done that I can go back to killing pigs.

What could Li Qing say? He reached out and picked up one of the paper lots.

The others did the same.

The last lot was left for Genbao, but as he started to open it, his hand shook and his palm turned sweaty, which slowed the process considerably, so slow in fact that before he saw what was inside his lot Zhuzi laughingly blurted out, Mine's black. I'm going to get my wife and child back! He laid his opened lot out in the center of the table, proving to the other three men that he'd picked the black bristle—about an inch in length, sort of shiny, shaped like a wheat awn, with a sharp point. As it lay inside the paper lot it emitted a slightly rank odor.

We have a winner, the youngster announced. You're

the town head's benefactor, and you three can go home and get some sleep.

Lame Zhao stared at the white bristle in his hand. Shit, he said. I'd have been better off home in bed. He tossed the lot and its bristle away.

With a glance at the black bristle on the table, Li Qing stood up and, without a word, headed to the door, giving the frame a vicious kick on his way out.

One by one they left, Genbao casting a backward glance at the signs proclaiming that the town head and Party secretary had spent nights in those guest rooms. He was tempted to speak to Butcher Li, but the man had his back to him as he gutted a butchered pig, so Genbao slipped silently out the gate.

Cool winds swept the ridge road, carrying with them the smell of new wheat from distant fields. Genbao breathed in deeply, all thoughts of sleep long gone.

Genbao's parents were nowhere in sight when he got home, where he was greeted by the aroma of freshly-baked bread, nice and oily. Inside the house he spotted a blue cloth bundle on a stool in the middle of the room. He went up and opened it. Not surprisingly, it contained the clothing and other items he'd need the next day when he left home to be the town head's benefactor: pants, shirt, shoes and socks, and, should he be gone more than a couple of weeks, summer T-shirts and a pair of shorts. She had even included cloth shoes with layered soles and rubber sneakers, obviously brand new. He wondered why she'd prepared so many shoes. Now, of course, he wouldn't be going anywhere, but even if he was lucky enough to be leaving to get married and wouldn't be back for ten days or a couple of weeks, there were more shoes in the bundle than he'd ever need.

Night had fallen as deeply as it ever would. Except for the continuing squeals at Butcher Li's house on the ridge, there were no sounds, not even from the moon as it passed overhead. The slightly pungent, soapy smell of new shoes and old clothes and the sweet smell of paste in the soles of the cloth shoes shimmered in the confined space. Genbao stood in front of the bundle for a moment before walking into the kitchen, where he went up to the counter. His mother had prepared dried provisions for him. The aroma of oily baked bread with onions and sesame oil poured from the counter down to the floor. Each of the baked items was as big as a griddle; cut into four equal slices, a total of twelve pie-shaped wedges was stacked in the middle of the counter.

He wept.

Genbao walked out into the yard and gazed to the west, where Zhuzi lived. There at sleepy Wu Family Slope he saw a row of new houses with tiled roofs, glinting blue in the night, dwarfing his own home, like a pile of dry straw lying fallow in a sea of lush grass. Disheartened by the contrast, he turned away from the sight and, to his surprise, was face to face with his neighbor to the east, who was, despite the lateness, walking spiritedly through the gate. I heard noise over here, Genbao, and I couldn't wait to run over. Your parents are at my place. I've got good news. My younger cousin, who was recently divorced, came to see me, and when she heard you were going to do prison time for the town head, and that you were still single, she agreed to the match right off. We waited at your place, but when you didn't show, we went home. And now, here you are. Your parents came over with her, and they had plenty to talk about. They want me to bring you over to meet my cousin. She's young and pretty, like a girl who's never been married. So, let's go. What are you waiting for? Why are you just standing there?

This neighbor, who had come to the village from town, had a lovely figure and a pretty face. She'd condescended to marry a man from Wu Family Slope when she saw what a good businessman he was. Formally educated, she was well-spoken and always looked good, no matter what she was wearing. Confidently aware that she was unique in the village, she saw no need to engage in give-and-take in her dealings with the local residents. She was like a school-teacher in a class of students. By this time the moon, which had migrated to a spot above the ridge, cast a veil over the yard where they were standing, so hazy that Genbao could not make out her face. All he could see was the willow-like movements of her arms as she spoke. Then she reached into the darkness and took his hand to lead him to her home. The softness of that hand reminded Genbao of warm cotton wrapping itself around his fingers. The feminine smell of her hair filled his nostrils, like the unexpected aroma of summer wheat on a cold winter day, and bursts of heated agitation rushed to his head like a herd of galloping horses. Little explosions went off inside his head as he tried to free his hand. He desperately wanted to tell her he wasn't going to do the prison time, after all, that the honor had gone to Zhuzi, who had chosen the right paper lot, but what emerged was, Don't tug on me like that, Aunty.

What's wrong? she said. Doesn't my cousin appeal to you?

Going to prison is nothing to be proud of, he said.

But you're doing it for the town head.

How do I know it'll only be for two or three weeks. The man died, after all, and I might have to stay in prison for six months or a year.

Still cocooned in haze, she laughed. You saw those three pairs of sneakers in the bundle, didn't you? My cousin went all the way to the purchasing co-op late at night to buy them for you. She said prisoners are made to work in brick kilns and factories, jobs that are especially hard on shoes. She said you'll be in prison for at least a year.

But what if it's two years, or three?

Nothing is more important to her than true feelings. She divorced her husband because he spent all his time in town womanizing. He cheated on her. It won't bother her that her man is in prison. What bothers her is a husband who spends all his money in hotels and public baths.

All right, Aunty, but what do I say to her?

Go get some of those baked onion breads your mother made and bring them over. Say you thought she might like a late-night snack.

So Genbao's neighbor left, walking quickly, like a goat prancing through tall grass. He watched as she stopped just beyond the gate and turned. Hurry, now. It'll be light soon, so get moving. She disappeared in the dark of night.

Rather than go into the kitchen for the late-night snack, as she'd suggested, he stood there thinking for a moment before following her out of the yard. But instead of heading to her house, he turned in the direction of the west end. Where was he going? To Zhuzi's house. It was one of those tall buildings, replete with a tiled roof and brick gateway, evidence that the occupants were well off. And yet his wife had run off with another man, a carpenter who also happened to be the younger brother of a branch secretary in a neighboring village. Genbao's arrival at Zhuzi's gate triggered a chorus of barking up and down the lane, which stopped abruptly when he reached the gate. Light filtering out through the seams came from an electric lamp. Obviously, Zhuzi was still awake, since right after breakfast, he and Butcher Li would be off to meet with the town head. He'd be taken by car to the county seat to check in with the police, and from there to prison for sentencing; many days would pass before he saw his home again. It hardly needs mentioning that he was inside packing for his stay in prison.

Genbao knocked lightly at the gate.

Rapping on the solid oak gate was like cracking his knuckles on a rock. In the darkness left behind by the moon's disappearance, the brittle sounds sailed beneath the village eaves like stones. But once they entered Zhuzi's house, they did not return; only barking dogs filled the silence.

Genbao knocked again, this time harder.

Who is it? Zhuzi called out.

It's me, Brother Zhuzi, Genbao.

Genbao? What do you want?

Open up, I need to talk to you.

Zhuzi came out into the yard, turned on the outdoor light, and threw open the double door.

Genbao fell immediately to his knees.

Zhuzi stumbled backward. What are you doing, Genbao? What's that for?

Good brother Zhuzi, Genbao said, let me go to prison for the town head. You at least have a wife and know what it's like to be a man. But I don't, and I'm almost thirty. If you let me take your place, the town head will want to know what he can do for my family, and the first thing I'll ask him to do is get your wife and child to come back home. What do you say?

Zhuzi just stared at Genbao, who was framed in the light. He said nothing.

So Genbao banged his head on the floor. Please, Zhuzi, I beg you.

If I let you take my place, Zhuzi said, do you promise you'll speak to the town head on my behalf?

If telling him to get your wife and child to come home isn't the first thing I say to him, I'll be a no-account rat.

Get up, Zhuzi said.

Genbao banged his head on the floor three more times before he got to his feet.

The rest of the night passed quickly

The early-morning sun rained its golden rays down on mid-spring fields, lighting up mountain valleys and ridges, trees and villages. When the residents of Wu Family Slope awoke, everyone knew that Genbao's house was the scene of a happy event. He was going to prison for the town head. His bundle was wrapped and ready, his bedding rolled and tied, his provisions—baked onion bread—were all tucked into his food pouch.

Genbao was going to be the town head's benefactor.

After a breakfast of sorghum porridge, salted vegetables, and oily rolls, he walked out with his belongings and got on the road under the gaze of fellow villagers—Li Qing, the cripple, Zhuzi, the couple who lived next door to the east, and her cousin. A betrothal had been arranged during the night. You definitely won't be coming back in a few weeks, she'd said, but I'll wait for you even if you're gone a year or two. She and her cousin were there to see him off when morning came. Unaware that she was Genbao's future wife, most of the villagers assumed she was just tagging along with her cousin to watch all the excitement. Genbao's father walked behind him, carrying his son's bedroll, pride and joy written on his face, like a man seeing his son off on a momentous journey. He'd left his pipe at home after deciding to replace it with filter cigarettes. Not actually smoking one, he merely let wisps of smoke rise from the lit end. Genbao's mother, who was carrying his food pouch, beamed when she spotted her future daughter-in-law, and Genbao saw a brief exchange between the two women, though he couldn't hear what they said. His future wife took the pouch from his mother and held her by the arm, like helping an old woman cross a bridge. She stood out from the crowd of onlookers like a summer flower in full bloom on a grassy slope. Like her cousin, she came from town, where she lived in a house separated only by a wall from the government offices, and where, as a child, she'd sometimes taken her food to eat; like her cousin, too, she had a cosmopolitan air—her dress, her speech, her behavior—that set her apart from the residents of Wu Family Slope. So when she took Genbao's mother by the arm, everyone knew what that meant and could not help feeling somewhat envious. No more than a dozen people had gathered at Genbao's gate at first, but by the time he and his parents came out and spoke briefly to their neighbors, the crowd had swelled dramatically. Some of the people, farmers on their way out to the fields, for instance, came rushing back to join the crowd of well-wishers when they heard that Genbao was to be the town head's benefactor. Don't forget your friends now that your future is bright, was the sort of thing they said. Forcing himself to take his eyes off his radiant wife to be, Genbao smiled and said, What do you mean, my future is bright? I'm heading off to prison! Who are you doing that for? the man asked. For the town head. He answered his own question. You're a life-saver, his life-saver. Don't kid yourself that I don't know what lies ahead for you.

Genbao merely smiled.

Slowly he threaded his way through the crowd that had gathered to send him off—people in front, people behind, laughter and footsteps sounding like leaves blowing in an autumn wind. Someone came up to his father, who was walking behind him, and offered to carry the bedroll. I can manage, he said as he let go of the bedroll, reached into his pocket and took out a fresh pack of cigarettes, which he opened and passed around, even sticking them into the mouths of those who refused his offer. Genbao wanted to get closer to Zhuzi, who was walking on the side of the road with Li Qing and the cripple, the three of them looking like best pals, as if the tense competition the night before had never occurred. But there were too many people, most of whom were trying to talk to him, so he could only wave and nod his head as a sign of apology and gratitude. The village had not witnessed such a happy, raucous send-off in a very long time; in the past, there had been occasions when one of the boys had joined the army, but never with such an outburst of public involvement, such an extravagant display of emotion. No, Genbao's departure was unique, and, as pride swelled inside him, he headed to the village entrance, stopping in front of the dining area to turn to wave the crowd away. Go on home, he said, that's far enough. I'm on my way to prison, not joining the army. But that had no effect on people who were intent on seeing him off properly.

The crowd stayed with him as he made his way to Butcher Li's house on the ridge.

The butcher himself was standing in bright sunlight waving to the crowd. Genbao quickened his pace, and the faster he walked, the more enthusiastically Butcher Li gestured, even cupping his hands around his mouth and shouting. But they were still too far away to hear him, although that did not stop the crowd from assuming he was urging Genbao to hurry up.

Which he did. Bundle in hand, he began trotting toward Butcher Li, not wanting to make the man wait too long. But he'd no sooner put some distance between himself and the crowd than the young butcher's helper from the night before appeared on the ridge and began running downhill toward him, the two of them destined to meet halfway. But then the youngster stopped next to a roadside boulder and shouted, You there, Liu Genbao, Butcher Li says not to come up, he says the town head called this morning to say he didn't need anyone to do prison time for him after all.

Genbao stopped running and stood like a utility pole in the middle of the road. What did you say? he shouted. What the hell are you saying?

You don't have to go, the youngster repeated. I mean, the parents of the guy who was killed were very understanding and don't blame the town head for the accident. They're not going to take him to court and they haven't demanded a big settlement. All they've asked is that he take the dead boy's younger brother as a sort of adopted son.

This time Genbao heard every word and felt as if his legs might not hold him up. Concentrating all his energy on his ankles to keep from crumpling to the ground, he gazed up at the ridge, where Butcher Li, whose back was to him, was directing, with considerable animation, some men who were loading a truck with butchered hogs. His powerful shoulders were as broad as a door.

Almost immediately, the raucous villagers who were giving him the grand send-off had caught up to him, like a man pulling a truck up a mountainside. Desperately wishing that Butcher Li or the youngster he'd sent down in his place would repeat the message for the benefit of the villagers, he walked slowly toward the ridge road.

The sun, which had climbed higher in the sky, was a bright, beautiful red.

Translated by Howard Goldblatt

Meijin, Baozi, and the White Kid
Shen Congwen

DESCRIBE TO ONE WHO has never known the taste of our pears from Pear Market village the sweetness of songs sung by girls of the White-faced Miao tribe, and you would be wasting your breath. Some people think the sound of sweeping oars beautiful. Others find beauty in the sound of the wind and the rain. Nor is there any dearth of simpletons who find it in a baby's cries at night or the sound of reeds as they whisper their dreams into

SHEN CONGWEN (1902–88), often called a "nativist" writer, wrote copiously, but not exclusively, about his native place, the remote mountainous region in the western part of Hunan, which is home to ethnic Miao and Tujia, as well as Han Chinese. From the 1920s to the 1940s Shen's lyrical, though not uncritical, portraits of rural China were at odds with the more politicized representations promoted on the left both in the 1930s and 1940s and after the communist revolution. This story (written in 1928) is a modern retelling of a local Miao/Tujia folktale. It captures the "imaginative nostalgia" Shen is often said to convey in his fictional depictions of his native region. Shen wrote most of his "nativist" fiction in Beijing, where he felt somewhat disenchanted with his fellow intellectuals and modern urban life in general and in reaction infused his native place with a kind of primitive vitality that he felt somehow lacking in the modern metropolis.

the breeze. All these are poetry. But the songs of the White-faced Miao girls are even more poetic, more apt to lead you to intoxicated rapture and to dream. Men who have heard their songs think nothing of shedding blood for these girls, such is their magic, handed down through history. Someone familiar with Miao legends could tell you fifty stories about famous, handsome men ensnared by ugly girls endowed with beautiful voices and fifty more about handsome men driven to distraction by the songs of girls from the White-faced tribe. And if, after all those, the tale-teller had yet another left to tell, the one forgotten would surely be the tale of Meijin.

The story goes like this. Meijin was a stunningly beautiful girl of the White-faced tribe. She and a boy from the Phoenix tribe, who was very handsome and of exemplary character, paired off while exchanging songs across mountain valleys. They expressed passionate love for each other in their songs; the girl proposed that the boy meet her that night in a cave. He who promised he would come was named Baozi. Baozi also meant to bring the girl a young mountain goat as a present, for it was the first time; he wanted to exchange a white kid for the red blood of her virginity. Even if their tryst was wrong, it was as if the gods themselves had given their assent. And yet, by nighttime, Baozi had forgotten all about it. After waiting for him all night long, Meijin froze to death in the cave for want of the warmth of a man. When Baozi, who slept at home until dawn, awoke and suddenly remembered, he hurried to the cave, only to find the girl already dead. So Baozi lay beside her and killed himself with his knife. Or, according to another version, he killed himself later on because he kept hearing Meijin singing and was unable to find her.

But all this was constructed from hearsay; what really happened was quite different. From a final poem that Baozi is said to have left before he died, written with a twig on the sandy floor of the cave, it seems to have been this way: Meijin was upset because Baozi failed to keep the appointment. She waited for him, but he did not come, and in the end, thinking she had been deceived, she killed herself. Baozi failed to keep the appointment because of the kid; when he did arrive, Meijin was already dead. That is why he pulled the knife from her chest and plunged it into his own, and he, too, fell lifeless in the cave. As to what happened afterward to the kid and why the hitherto always trustworthy Baozi became such a faithless lover, you would have to ask the kid. It was all because of the kid that what was to have been joyous turned into a tragedy. It is no wonder that even today the White-faced Miao do not eat goat meat.

But if you wanted to question the kid, where would you go? Lovers today still offer their mistresses a small white kid, and, to express their loyalty and the strength of their love, they always say that the kid is descended from the one Baozi brought for Meijin all those years ago though in truth, even whether the original kid was male or female no one can really say now.

Just let me set down what I know. The source of my story is the robber Wu Rou, a descendant of the man who took the kid that Baozi and Meijin left behind and who also was Baozi's martial arts instructor. What has come down from him is naturally likely to be more reliable. This is the story:

With Meijin standing on the southern mountain slopes and Baozi on the northern, they sang from morning till night. It was on the slopes known today as the Mountain of Singing. In those days it was called the Mountain of Wild Chrysanthemums, for the flowers ran riot there, covering the whole hillside with a sheet of yellow in autumn. Yellow flowers cover the mountain yet today, but it has been renamed because of what happened to Meijin. In her song Meijin finally admitted defeat and that she must by rights give herself to Baozi, to do with as he wished. She sang:

> *It is only by letting the autumn wind have its way*
> *with them that the red leaves may fly over the*
> *mountain.*
> *It is by you alone that I shall be made a woman.*

Baozi was filled with delight to hear this song. He knew that he had won—that the heart of the most beautiful and enticing girl in all the White-faced tribe now belonged to him. And so he replied:

> *You who are renowned among the Miao as the fair-*
> *est of all,*
> *Please go to Precious Stone Cave by Huang village,*
> *And when the great stars above gaze at one another*
> *in the sky,*
> *That's when I'll see you, and you'll see me.*

Meijin sang back to him:

> *Oh my beloved wind, I shall do whatever you wish.*
> *All I want is that your heart should be as bright as*
>   *the sun.*
> *All I want is for your warmth to melt me, like the*
>   *sun's heat.*
> *Give no one cause to jest that the Phoenix tribe's*
>   *finest man is faithless,*
> *And forget not what it is that you have asked me to do.*

Baozi sang back:

> *Rest easy, greatest goddess of my heart.*
> *Thine own eyes have witnessed the beauty of the*
>   *"leopard."*
> *And others universally bear witness to his*
>   *faithfulness.*
> *Though the time comes that it begins to rain knives,*
> *I shall flinch from nothing to reach your side and*
>   *kiss you.*

It grew dark. Wild Chrysanthemum Mountain was wreathed in purple mist as it is still today at dusk. A few red clouds filled the sky, billowing to see the sun off on its downward journey, and the sun bade them farewell. This was the time for woodcutters to go home and herdsmen to return their sheep and cattle to the pens, for the day was at an end. The people who led this peaceful life had turned over another page, without any need to ask what was on the next, for this was the time to come down from the mountains, return from the rivers, and go home from the fields; it was the time to come home to the evening meal.

After whistling to wish Meijin farewell, Baozi hurried home, intending to find a newborn kid after his meal and take it to Precious Stone Cave for the meeting with his lover. Meijin too went home.

When Meijin had gone home and had something to eat, she changed into fresh undergarments, rubbed her body with sweet-smelling oils, and powdered her face. Then, in front of a bronze mirror, she did her hair up into a big coil and wound a sixteen-foot silk scarf around it. When she was quite ready, she set off for Precious Stone Cave with a long necked gourd full of wine, an embroidered purse full of coins, and a sharp little dagger.

Precious Stone Cave was then as it is today. It was dry, with a floor of fine white sand, a bed and benches made of stone, a fireplace, and a natural hole through which you could see the stars. The only difference is that then it was a bridal chamber for Meijin and Baozi and today it has become a sacred place. The age of Meijin and Baozi has passed. Good customs, like lovely women, wither in time. This cave, safe from the chills and the heat, this wonderful place just made for young lovers, is now a place to worship gods. Though it is said that these gods are none other than those two young people who died for love, if the souls of Meijin and Baozi are with us, they must surely regret that this cave has been taken over for such a purpose. No use could be more fitting for such a beautiful place, as a memorial to the lovers who died there, than to furnish it as a meeting place especially for young men and women who have fallen in love through song. But, as I said, the good customs of this area have died out, the passions of its people have declined, and the women are slowly becoming more like Chinese women. Their affections have shifted to empty and meaningless things like cattle and sheep, gold and silver, so that the importance of love has clearly deteriorated. Beautiful songs and beautiful bodies alike have been supplanted by material things and are no longer valued. Meijin and Baozi probably could not tolerate such false warmth and empty love, even in this fine place. Better, then, to let it be a place of worship after all than have it sullied by the "love" of modern times.

But let me tell you what it was like when Meijin went to Precious Stone Cave.

She came early, to wait for Baozi. Once in the cave, she sat on the edge of the bed, which was hewn from a great blue rock. This was to be her bridal bed. It was spread with straw, and there was a bundle of straw for a pillow. The vaulted cave roof, with its dry, crisp air, was like a canopy, so that this bed seemed much better than most real ones.

She hung the calabash of wine from a wall hook and put the embroidered purse beside the pillow (she had prepared them both for Baozi), and then she waited in the darkness for her young and handsome lover. The mouth of the cave was faintly illuminated from outside; she sat there gazing at the light, waiting for the time when Baozi's massive shadow would appear.

To amuse herself, she softly sang to herself all the songs she knew. With them she praised the valor of the leopard in the mountains and the beauty of her leopard among men. She described her feelings at this time and how

Baozi must be feeling. She ran her hands over every part of her body and smelled herself just as thoroughly. Everywhere she touched was rounded and smooth as silk and butter, and all the fragrances she smelled were sweet. She unfurled her turban and undid the coil of her hair, letting it fall free and spread, blacker than the night, down to the very ground. She was the most beautiful girl in her tribe. Of all men, only Baozi was fit to possess her body.

Her body was round and filled out, with curves everywhere, yet it was also very slender and well proportioned. Her perfect round face was set with a tiny mouth, a fine, straight nose, a pointed chin, and long, long eyebrows. It was as though her mother had molded her along the lines of the Fairy Lady He, for among mortals there could never be such a model of perfection. Just think how moving was this scene: in an hour or two she would take off all her clothes and become a bride—a girl like her, in a place like this, and yet a little shy to think of this momentous event, when she would take up all the passion and all the strength of a fiery young male.

Even a writer born in the twentieth century and plying his trade in Shanghai, 1928, an expert at digging up dirt about his friends and spreading rumors—an acclaimed litterateur with a gilded tongue, of acknowledged intelligence and wit—even he would be hard pressed to imagine the beauty of Meijin that night.

The elegance and purity of the girls of the White-faced Miao are long gone since the time of Meijin. We can all believe that. The girls you see today are far, far inferior, yet even so they turn the heads of countless males and make self-respecting Han Chinese hang their heads; from this, you may get some idea of Meijin's beauty.

Long sullied now by many vile and false desires, the word *love* can never regain the purity of a prior age. We shall not use the currently fashionable words to try to elaborate on Meijin's feelings at the time; we shall say only that her heart was pounding as she waited for Baozi to come and lie with her: she did not sigh or soliloquize, as your average literary genius might imagine!

She hoped only that Baozi would come soon, and, though she knew that leopards bite, she was quite happy to be devoured.

But where was her leopard?

There was no kid in Baozi's home, so he went to buy one from the old chieftain in the village. Bringing with him four strings of copper cash for the purchase of a young female kid with a white coat, Baozi explained what it was he needed the moment he entered the chieftain's gate.

When he heard that Baozi had come for a kid, and realized that a happy event was imminent, the chieftain asked, "Whose bridegroom will you be tonight, my fine young fellow?"

Baozi said, "*Your* eyes, Uncle, can see who is to be Baozi's bride this night."

"No one but the camellia goddess is fit to share Baozi's home. None but the fairy of Big Ghost Cave is fit to love and be loved by him. Which mortal woman could it be? I do not know."

"Uncle, though all call Baozi of the Phoenix tribe handsome, he is unworthy to be the footrest of this bride."

"Do not be so modest, young man. When he surrenders to a woman, a man always sees himself as worthless by comparison to her."

"How true, Uncle! When I am with her, I cannot talk about myself. I beg your pardon, Uncle, but tonight I shall become a man, and I simply cannot express what my heart feels about her. I have come here to see if you could spare a kid that I might take and give to this goddess in return for her blood."

The chieftain was an old man who could see the future and read a person's fortune in his face. He gave a start when Baozi mentioned blood in connection with the happy event to come, sensing that it did not augur well. He said, "Young man, there is something wrong about the way you look."

"Of course I would not look the same today as I usually do, Uncle."

"Come into the light, and let me look at you."

Baozi turned his face toward the big tung-oil lamp as the old man commanded. The chieftain looked at Baozi, and nodded his head, but said nothing.

Baozi said, "Uncle, you can see things so clearly—can you tell whether the omens are good or bad?"

"Young man, knowledge is just a kind of pastime for old people; it is of no use to you! Now, if you want a kid, go to the pen, and choose one that you like. No need to give me any money, and no need for any thanks. Tomorrow I would like to see you and your bride —"

He stopped talking and led Baozi round to the pen behind the house. The chieftain held the lamp while Baozi searched among the goats for the one he wanted. There were close to fifty goats in the pen, of which half were kids, but, search as he might, there was not one he liked. The pure white ones were too big, and the smaller ones looked rather mottled. A big one would naturally be unsuitable, and one with an impure coat would not make a fitting present for Meijin, either.

"Any of them will do, young man; just pick one."

"I am trying."

"Are none of them suitable?"

"Uncle, I simply cannot compare my bride's spotless virtue to a kid with a patchy coat."

"Take any one at all, and go quickly to your bride."

"I cannot go empty handed, and I cannot take any of your kids, Uncle, so I had better go look elsewhere."

"Please, simply pick one."

"Thank you, Uncle, but this is the first time I have ever made a promise to a woman; I cannot make do with an ordinary kid."

"But I tell you, it will be all right even if you bring nothing. It is not good to make your bride wait. What she wants is not the kid."

"I know you mean well, Uncle, but I have made a promise to my bride." Baozi thanked the chieftain and set off to look for a kid elsewhere.

The chieftain saw Baozi off at the gate and sighed as he watched the boy vanish rapidly into the darkness. The seer could do nothing, for what was to happen had been predetermined. He could only close the gate and wait for news. Baozi went to five houses, but none of them had a suitable kid—either they were too big, or their coats were not pure white. A good kid was as hard to find in this place as a good woman, and it would only be by chance that he might find one that he liked.

By the time Baozi emerged from the fifth house where goats were raised, the sky was full of stars, and all was quiet. He thought, if I cannot keep my very first promise to my girl, how will I ever win her trust? If I go empty handed, saying it is because I searched the whole village but could not find a kid I liked, she will know that I am lying. So he decided that he must search the whole village.

He went and knocked at the gates of all the families he knew, and, when the gates were opened, he quietly told them that he wanted a kid. He was known to all the villagers for his strength and good looks, and, when they heard that he wanted a kid to give to his girl, they were all very keen to help. They led him to their pens to look at their goats, just as kindly and patiently as had the chieftain, for Baozi was a fellow villager. But he looked at them all, and strangely enough not a single kid was to his liking.

He had not forgotten that Meijin would be anxiously awaiting him in the cave. Her request to him as he left, that he should come when the stars came out, still rang in his ears. But, having promised his sweetheart a little kid, he was now very anxious that he had no found one, and, in the search, he had forgotten the rime.

He decided that, since he could not find a pure white kid in this village, if he really wanted one, he must go to another village a mile away and look there. He gazed up at the sky and judged that there was still time. Thus, to keep his word, Baozi went straight to the other village to buy the kid.

The way to the village was very familiar to him. He had gone but a few hundred yards when he heard the sound of a kid bleating in the grass beside the road. The sound was very low and faint, but he knew a, once that it came from a kid. Baozi stopped. He listened carefully, and the kid bleated again, very softly. He realized it must have fallen into a deep pit by the roadside. Having been there all day by itself, it was crying miserably in the dark, missing its mother and feeling homesick.

Parting the grass by starlight, Baozi saw an opening in the ground. The kid bleated again on hearing the grass stir; its feeble sound rose up through the hole. Baozi was delighted. Knowing that the weather had been fair lately and that the pit must be dry, he slid down into the hole. It was only as deep as his waist, with a bottom that was indeed solid and dry. In a moment Baozi saw the kid, which started bleating all the more piteously, though it did not approach him. It was newborn, not ten days old, with a foreleg broken from the fall, probably caused by a goatherd who had carelessly driven his flock across the pit.

Baozi cradled the injured kid in his arms as he climbed out of the pit. Thinking that he would have to use this one in any case, he set out toward Precious Scone Cave and his tryst with Meijin. But the kid kept bleating softly as they went. Realizing that it was in pain, Baozi felt he must carry it to the home of the village chieftain and ask him to dress it with some ointment before he took it to the cave. So he turned back and went to the chieftain's house.

Baozi knocked at the door. The old man, unable to sleep

for worrying about the boy, thought that the bad news about him had arrived. He asked who it was, through the door.

"It is your nephew, Uncle. I have found a kid, but the poor little thing is hurt; it has a broken leg. I have come to ask you to heal it."

"Have you not gone to your bride yet, young man? It is already midnight. Leave the kid here, and do not delay a second longer."

"Uncle, I am certain my bride will love this kid. I cannot see the color of its coat properly, but, when I was carrying it, I felt sure it must be pure white! It is as gentle and soft as my bride, and its —"

The chieftain was alarmed to hear the young fellow waxing so lyrical about an injured kid he had just happened to pick up. He drew back the bolt with a thud and opened the door. A ray of light from his lamp fell on the kid in Baozi's arms, and Baozi could see the color of its coat. It was as white as the snow on Dali. Baozi quickly lifted it up and kissed it.

"Young man, what are you doing? Have you forgotten that tonight you are to be a bridegroom?"

"I have not forgotten, Uncle! This kid is a gift from heaven. Please, quickly rub some ointment on its leg so that I may carry it to my bride."

Shaking his head, the chieftain took the kid in his arms and examined it by the light of the lamp. The kid stopped bleating when it saw the lamplight. It only closed its eyes and snorted.

Soon after, Baozi was on his way to Precious Stone Cave, the kid sleeping peacefully in his arms. He longed to see his Meijin there and to tell how heaven had sent this kid. Taking long strides without ever resting, he ascended the hill, crossing countless high cliffs and ravines as he went, until he came to Precious Stone Cave. By the time he reached the mouth of the cave, the eastern sky was getting light. The heavens were full of stars, and their light shone on the entrance to the cave. It was cold and desolate inside. He could see no one.

He called our softly, "Meijin, Meijin, Meijin!"

He walked a little way inside and was met not by a voice but by a smell from the interior of the cave. He recognized it at once as the stench of blood. Stunned, he stood there for a moment like an idiot, then flung the kid to the ground and ran inside.

He went to the bed. In a few moments, with the faint gleam of starlight coming through the open roof, he made out the shape of Meijin lying on the bed. The smell of blood was coming from her. He rushed over and felt her forehead, her face, her mouth: her mouth and nose were still slightly warm.

"Meijin! Meijin!"

He called her name several times before she managed a faint response.

"What have you done?"

He listened to her breathing, which seemed to come not from her mouth but from her belly. At last she turned toward him, wanting to raise herself but not having the strength.

She said, quietly and haltingly, "You who call out to me, are you the one who sang to me in the daytime?"

"Yes, my love! The one who always sang so sadly during

the day and was so alone in bed at night; but now, today, that boy has come to be your bridegroom.—What has happened? Why are you like this?"

"Why?"

"Yes, who has done this to you?"

"It is that faithless boy from the Phoenix tribe; he lied to me. Even the most handsome, perfect boy must have a fault, so the gods made him capable of lying. I did not want to be deceived by a liar. And now it is over for me."

"No, no! You are wrong! It was all because the boy from the Phoenix tribe did not wish to break his first promise to the girl. He went and searched the whole night, until by chance he came upon the promised kid. Now he has found the kid but lost the girl. Oh heaven, tell me how I should have kept my word!"

When the dying Meijin heard this, she realized that Baozi was late because he had searched for the kid, not because he had broken his vow. She realized that she had been wrong to give up hope and plunge the knife into her breast. She asked Baozi to take her up and lay her head against his chest so that he might kiss her on the forehead.

She said, "I am dying. . . . When it grew light and still you had not come, I thought myself deceived. . . . And so I stabbed myself with this knife. You wanted my blood, and here it is. I do not hate you. . . . Pull out the knife, and let me die. . . . Run, escape beyond the mountains before it gets completely light, for you are innocent of my death."

Baozi wept silently as he listened to her speak in fits and starts about her death. He thought a moment and touched her gently. Her breasts were wet with blood, and between them was the bloody handle of the knife. His heart went cold. He shuddered.

She said, "Baozi, why do you not do as I ask? You told me that the whole of you belonged to me. So do as I say, and pull the knife out, to save me from suffering any more."

Still Baozi said nothing.

In a little while she spoke again.

"Baozi, I understand now. Do not be sad. Bring the kid, and let me see it."

He laid her down again very carefully and left the cave to get the kid. He had unthinkingly hurled the poor thing on the ground. It lay there panting, half dead.

Baozi looked up at the sky, which was now completely light. Far away, a cock crowed. He heard waterwheels in the distance—sounds he usually sensed while dreaming.

He carried the kid into the cave and put it near Meijin's breast. "Lift me up, Baozi; let me kiss the kid you have brought."

With his arm around her shoulders he raised her up and put her hand on the kid. "How sad that it has been hurt, too. Take it away now. . . . Pull out the knife, my love. Do not cry. . . . I know you love me, and I do not hate you for what you have done. Run away now with the kid; make your getaway. . . . Oh, you fool, what are you doing?"

Baozi had bared his own breast and was pulling at the knife. It was lodged so deep inside her that he had to use great force to remove it. Her blood gushed out and spattered him all over. Then he thrust the bloody knife into his own chest. Meijin saw this. She died with a smile on her face.

After it got light, the chieftain led some villagers to Precious Stone Cave to look for the couple. They found the two dead bodies, the half-dead kid that the old man had earlier anointed with his own hands, and a song that Baozi must have written with a twig in the sand just before he died. The chieftain committed the song to memory and carried the kid home with him.

Nowadays, the women of the White-faced Miao are no longer filled with such passion. They can still forgive men, they can still sacrifice themselves for them, and they can still sing songs to stir the soul. But they cannot do as Meijin did.

Translated by Caroline Mason

The Old Gun

Mo Yan

AS HE SWUNG THE GUN down from his right shoulder with his index-finger-less right hand, he was caught in a ray of golden sunlight. The sun was sinking rapidly in a smooth shallow arc; fragmentary sounds like those of a receding tide rippled from the fields, along with an air of desolation by turns pronounced and faint. Gingerly he placed the gun on the ground among the patches of coin-shaped moss, feeling a sense of distress as he saw how damp the earth was. The long-barreled, homemade mus-

MO YAN (1955–) leapt onto the literary scene in China with the publication of his novel *Red Sorghum* (1986), subsequently made into a film by Zhang Yimou. Since then, he has published numerous novels and short stories, many of which have been translated into English by Howard Goldblatt, his long-time collaborator. Much of Mo Yan's fiction, including the present story, is set in his native Gaomi county in Shadong province—a real place, but one obviously enhanced and mythicized in Mo Yan's fictional representations—and is said to exemplify the "searching for roots" literary movement. Like much of Mo Yan's fiction, this story (written in 1985) expresses a desire for a lost world, a world that possessed a vitality and machismo lacking in the present. This desire for a lost past is conveyed allegorically in the story through the boy's relationship with his father's gun.

ket, its butt mahogany, lay unevenly on the soggy ground; beside it the evening sun picked out a fallen sorghum ear on which a great cluster of delicate, tender golden shoots had sprouted, casting discoloring shadows onto the black gun-barrel and deep-red butt. He took the powder-horn from around his waist, at the same time slipping off his black jacket to reveal a raw-boned torso. He wrapped the gun and the powder-horn in the jacket and lay them on the ground, then took three paces forward. Bending down, he stretched out his sun-drenched arms and dragged out one sheaf from among the great clump of sorghum stalks.

The autumn floods had been heavy and the land, water-logged for thousands of hectares, looked like an ocean. In the water the sorghum held high its crimson heads; whole platoons of rats scurried across them as nimbly as birds in flight. By harvest time the water was at chest height, and the people waded in and took the ears of sorghum away on rafts. Red-finned carp and black-backed grass carp appeared from nowhere to dart about among the green aerial roots of the sorghum stalks. Now and again an emerald green kingfisher shot into the water, then shot back out with a tiny glistening fish in its beak. In August the flood waters gradually subsided, revealing roads covered in mud. On the low-lying land the water remained, forming pools of all shapes and sizes. The cut sorghum stalks could not be hauled away; they were dragged out of the water and stacked on the road or on the higher ground around the edges of the pools. A glorious sunlight shone on the low-lying plains. For miles around there was hardly a village; the pools sparkled; the clumps of sorghum stood like clusters of blockhouses.

Silhouetted against the bright warm sun and a big expanse of water, he dragged aside sheaf after sheaf of sorghum, piling them up at the edge of the pool until he had made a square hide half a man's height. Then he picked up the gun, jumped into the hide, and sat down. His head came just level with the top of the hide. From outside he was invisible, but through the holes he had left he could clearly see the pool and the sand-bar which rose in its middle like a solitary island; he could see the rosy sky and the brown earth, too. The sky seemed very low; the sun's rays daubed the surface of the water a deep red. The pool stretched away into the hazy dusk, sparkling brilliantly, darts of radiance dancing around its edge like a ring of warm eyelashes. On the sand-bar in the pool, by now a pale shade of blue, clumps of yellow reeds stood solemnly upright. The sand-bar itself, surrounded by flickering light, seemed gently adrift. The hazier the surroundings grew, the brighter the water gleamed, and the more pronounced the impression that the sand-bar was drifting—he felt that it was floating toward him, floating nearer, until it was only a few steps away and he could have jumped onto it. They still hadn't arrived on the sandbar; he gazed uneasily at the sky once more, thinking, it's about time, they ought to be here by now.

He had no idea where they came from. That day the workers had spent the whole afternoon shifting sorghum stalks. When the team leader said it was time to put down tools, the men headed for home by the dozen, their long shadows swaying as they went. He had rushed over here to relieve himself when suddenly he caught sight of them. It was as though he had been punched in the chest—his heart faltered for a moment before it resumed beating. His eyes were dazzled by the great flock of wild ducks landing on the sand-bar. Every night for two weeks he hid among the sorghum sheafs watching them; he observed that they always arrived, cawing loudly, at around this time of the evening, as if they had come flying from beyond the sky. Before landing they would circle elegantly above the pool, like a great gray-green cloud now unfurling, now rolling back . . . When they descended onto the sand-bar, their wings beating the air, he was beside himself with excitement. Never before had he come across so many wild ducks on such a small piece of land, never . . .

They still weren't here—by now they really should have been. They weren't here yet . . . or they weren't coming? He was feeling anxious, even began to suspect that what he had seen before had been just an illusion—all along he had never quite believed there could really be such a large flock of wild ducks in this place. He had often heard the old people in the village telling tales of heavenly ducks, but the ducks in the stories were always pure white, and this flock of wild ducks was not. The ones with pretty green feathers on their heads and necks, a white ring round their throats and wings like blue mirrors—weren't they drakes? Those with golden-brown bodies, dappled with dark brown markings—weren't they females? They certainly weren't heavenly ducks, for they left little green and brown feathers all over the sand-bar. He felt greatly reassured at the sight of these feathers. He sat down, picked up his jacket and shook it open, revealing the gun and the shiny powder-horn. The gun lay peacefully on top of the sorghum stalks, its body gleaming dark red, almost the color of rust. In the past red rust had covered it several times and had eaten away at the metal, leaving it pocked and pitted. Now, though, there was no rust—he had sandpapered it all away. The gun lay there twisted like a hibernating snake; at any moment, he felt, it might wake up, fly into the air, and start thrashing the sorghum stalks with its steel tail. When he stretched out his hand to touch the gun, his first sensation was an iciness in his fingertips, and the chill spread to his chest and made him shiver for a long while. The sun was sinking faster now, its shape altering all the while, flattening out and distorting, like a semi-fluid sphere hitting a smooth steel surface. Its underside was a flat line, its curved surfaces under extreme tension; at last they burst and the bubbling icy red liquid meandered away in every direction. A trance-like calm descended on the pool as the crimson liquid seeped down, turning its depths into a thick red broth, while the surface remained crystal clear and blindingly bright. Suddenly, he caught sight of a gold-hooped dragonfly suspended from a tall, withered blade of grass, its bulging eyes like purple gems, turning now to the left, now to the right, refracting light as they did so.

He reached for the gun and laid it across his legs, its body stretching out behind him along the right-angle of his thighs and belly; the barrel peeped out from beneath his chin at the pale gray southern sky. He opened the lid of the powder-horn, then pulled from his pocket a long, thin measuring cylinder which he filled with gunpowder. He poured this measure into the gun barrel; the smooth sound it made as it fell echoed from the muzzle. He then took a pinch of iron shot from a small iron box and tipped it into the muzzle of the gun; from inside the barrel there came a clatter. Now he pulled out a long rod from below the barrel and tamped down the mixture of gunpowder and shot with its uneven head. He moved as gingerly as if he were scratching a drowsy tiger's itch, nerve-ends tingling, heart pounding. As soon as he had put the third measure of gun-powder and the third handful of shot into the barrel, an icy cold clutched him; beads of cold sweat broke out on his forehead. His hands were trembling as he took out the cottonwool stopper he had prepared for the purpose and plugged the mouth of the gun. He felt starving, his whole body limp. He snapped a piece of grass from the ground, rubbed the mud from it, put it into his mouth and began to chew on it, but this only made his hunger worse. . . .

Just then, though, he heard the whistle of wings beating the air above the water-flats. He had to hurry and complete his final task of preparation: attaching the percussion cap. He pulled back the protruding head of the hammer, revealing a nipple-shaped protuberance connected to the gun barrel. There was a round groove in the top of the protuberance with a tiny hole in its center. With great care he tore away several layers of paper from around the golden percussion cap, then fitted it into this groove. The percussion cap contained yellow gunpowder; as soon as the hammer struck it, this would explode, igniting the powder in the barrel and sending a fiery snake leaping from the muzzle, slender at first, then bigger until finally the gun looked like an iron broom. This gun had hung on the pitch-black gable in their house for so long that he had learned the mystery of its workings as if by revelation. Two days before, when he took it down and rubbed it clean of the rust which pocked its surface, he was actually completely at ease with it.

The wild ducks were here. At first they circled a hundred meters up in the air, wings beating. They dived and climbed, merged, then scattered again, hurtling down from all directions to skim across the sparkling surface of the reddened water. He got to his knees, holding his breath, eyes glued to the circle upon circle of purple radiance. Gently he edged the barrel of the gun through the gap in the sorghum stalks, heart pounding crazily. The wild ducks were still whirling around in circles of ever-changing size; it was almost as if the water-flats were spinning with them. Several times, some of the green-feathered drakes almost flew straight into the muzzle of his gun; he caught a glimpse of their pale green beaks and the gleam of cunning in their black eyes. The sun had grown wider and flatter still, turning black around the edges, its center still like molten iron, crackling and spitting sparks.

The ducks suddenly started calling, the "quack quack quack" of the drakes merging with the "quack quack quack" of the females in a great cacophony. He knew they were about to land—after observing them minutely for a dozen days now he knew they always cried out just before they landed. It was only a few moments, since their silhouettes had first appeared in the sky, but already he felt as if an extremely long time had passed; the violent cramps in his stomach reminded him again of his hunger. At last the ducks descended, only extending their purple legs and stretching their wings out flat when they were almost on the ground. Their snowy tails fluffed out like feathery fans, they hit the ground at such speed that the momentum made them stagger a couple of paces. Suddenly the mud was no longer brown: countless suns shimmered in the ducks' brilliant plumage as the entire flock waddled to and fro, carrying the sunlight with it.

Stealthily he raised the gun, rested the butt on his shoulder, and trained the muzzle on the increasingly dense pack of ducks. Another piece had vanished from the sun, which looked distorted, bizarre. Some of the wild ducks had settled on the ground, some were standing, some flew a little way then landed again. It's time, he thought, I should open fire, but he didn't do it. As he ran his hand over the trigger he suddenly realized his great disadvantage, recalling with a sense of pain his index finger: two of the joints were missing, the last one alone remained, a gnarled tree stump squatting between his thumb and his middle finger.

He was only six years old when his mother came back from his father's funeral, dressed in mourning—a long white cotton gown with a hempen cord tied around the waist, her hair flowing loose. Her eyelids were so swollen they were transparent, her eyes merely narrow slits from which her tear-stained, darkling gaze flashed out. She called out his name: "Dasuo, come here." He approached her with trepidation. She grabbed hold of his hand and gulped twice, craning her neck as though trying to swallow something hard. "Dasuo, your dad's died, do you realize that?" she said. He nodded, and heard her carry on, "Your dad's died. When you die you can never come back to life, do you realize that?" He gazed perplexedly at her, nodding energetically all the while. "You know how your dad died?" she asked. "He was shot with this gun; this gun was handed down from your grandmother. You're never to touch it: I'm going to hang it on the wall; you're going to look at it every day. And when you look at it you should think of your father, and study hard so you can live a decent life and bring a bit of credit to your ancestors." He wasn't sure how well he understood his mum's words, but he carried on nodding energetically.

And so the gun hung in their house on the gable, which was stained black and shiny by the smoke of decades. Every day he saw it. Later, when he went up from first to second grade, his mum hung a paraffin lamp on the gable every evening to give him enough light to study by. Whenever he saw the black characters in the books his head started spinning, and he couldn't help thinking of the gun and the story behind it. The wind off the desolate plain seeped through the lattice window, buffeting the flames in the oil lamp; the flames looked like the head of a writing brush, with wisps of black smoke shimmering at its tip. Though he appeared intent on his books, he was always aware of the spirit of the gun; he even seemed to hear it clicking. He felt like you do when you see a snake—wanting to look but scared at the same time. The gun hung there, barrel pointing down, butt upward, a gloomy black glow emanating from its body. The powder-horn hung along-side, tangled up with it, its slender waist resting against the hammer. It was red-gold in color, its big end facing downward, its small end upward. How high the gun and the powder-horn hung, how beautiful they looked hanging there—an ancient gun and an ancient powder-horn hanging on an ancient gable, tormenting his soul.

One evening he climbed up on a high stool and took the gun and the powder-horn down. Holding them up to the lamp-light, he inspected them carefully; the leaden weight of the gun in his hands brought him an acute sense of grief. Just at this moment, his mum walked in from the other room. She was not yet forty, but her hair was already gray, and she said: "Dasuo, what are you doing?" He just stood there blankly, the gun in one hand and the powder-horn in the other. "Where did you come in your class exams?" she asked him. "Second from bottom," he replied. "You good-for-nothing! Hang that gun back up!" He replied stubbornly, "No, I want to go and kill . . ." His mum slapped him round the face and said, "Hang it up. The only thing you're going to do is get on with your studies, and don't you forget it." He hung the gun on the wall. His mum went over to the stove, picked up a chopper, and told him calmly, "Hold out your index finger." He stretched it out obediently. She pressed the finger onto the edge of the *kang;* he began to squirm with fear. "Don't move," she told him. "Now remember this, you're never to touch that gun again." She raised the chopper . . . it fell in a flash of cold steel, a violent jolt surged from his fingertips up to his shoulders, his vertebrae arched with the strain. Blood oozed slowly from the severed finger. His mother was weeping as she staunched the wound with a handful of lime. . . .

As he looked at the stub of his finger with its single joint, his nose began to twitch. How many days had he gone without meat now? Couldn't remember exactly; but he could distinctly remember all the meat he had eaten in the past. He seemed never to have eaten his fill of meat.

The first time he caught sight of those plump wild ducks, meat was the first thing he thought of. The next thing he thought of was the gun—he had come out in goose-pimples all over as he recalled how his mum had chopped off his finger at the joint because of it. But in the end, yesterday afternoon, he had taken the gun down. Its body was covered in dust, as thick as a coin, and it was enmeshed from top to bottom in a tangle of spider's webs. The leather strap, chewed through by insects, snapped as soon as he touched it. There was still a lot of gunpowder in the horn—when he poured it out to dry he discovered a golden percussion cap. He picked up this single percussion cap, hands trembling with excitement. The first thing that came into his mind was his father: he felt how lucky he was, for where would you get one of these percussion caps nowadays? . . . I haven't got any money, even if I had some I still wouldn't be able to get a meat coupon; I'm thick, even if I wasn't I still wouldn't get a chance to go to school, and anyway what use would it be? Looking at the stump of his finger, he tried to console himself. His mum had only chopped off the tip, but afterward the wound had turned septic and he had lost another section—hence its present state. As he thought of all these things, he became filled with hatred for this flock of wild ducks with all their fine feathers. I'm going to kill you, kill the lot of you if it's the last thing I do! Then I'll eat you, chew your bones to a pulp and swallow them down. He imagined how crispy and aromatic their bones must be. He stretched his middle finger into the trigger guard.

Still he didn't pull the trigger. This was because another gaggle of wild ducks was swirling down from the sky in another spinning cloud of color. There was a great commotion among the ducks on the sand-bar. Some stamped their feet, some took off; it was hard to tell whether they were expressing welcome or anger toward their fellows. He gazed irritably at the flurry of birds and gently withdrew the gun. The sun had grown pointed like a sweet potato, its rays now dark green and brilliant purple. The ducks' activity startled the gold-hooped dragonfly into flight. It skimmed low across the surface of the water and came to rest on his hide, its six legs clamped fast to a sorghum leaf, its long golden-hooped tail dangling down. He saw the two bright beads of light in its eyes. The flock of wild ducks was gradually regrouping and growing calmer. On the water's surface, shattered by their claws, concentric ripples spread out, creating new ripples where they collided.

The two flocks of ducks had merged into one. If I had a big net, he thought, and suddenly flung it over them . . . but he knew he had no net, just a gun. Gingerly he removed the percussion cap, pulled out the cotton wool stopper, and poured three more measures of gunpowder and three more measures of shot into the muzzle. . . . Once more he took aim at the ducks, his heart filled with a primitive blood-lust . . . Such a huge flock of ducks, such a slender gun barrel . . . He edged stealthily back once more and poured another two cylinders of gunpowder into the muzzle, then plugged it again. The barrel was almost full now, and when he lifted the gun up he felt how heavy it was. His trembling middle finger pressed on the trigger—at the split second of firing he closed his eyes.

The head of the hammer struck the golden percussion cap with a click, but no shot rang out. The rings on the water's surface seemed to be slowly contracting; the purple vapor which hung between heaven and earth was denser than ever, the red glow fading fast, the brightness of the water's surface undiminished but gradually assuming a deeper hue. Clustered together, the ducks looked so solid, beautiful, warm, their soft, clean plumage dazzling. Their cunning eyes seemed to be staring disdainfully at the muzzle of his gun, as if in mockery of his impotence. He took out the percussion cap, glancing at the mark left on the firing plate by the hammer. A warm breath of putrid air wafted over from the flock of ducks; their bodies gave off a soft, smooth sound as they rubbed against each other. He replaced the percussion cap, not believing that this could really have happened. Dad, Granny, hadn't it fired for them at the first attempt? It was ten or more years since his dad died, but his story was still common currency in the village. He could dimly recall a very tall man with a pitted face and yellow whiskers.

His dad's story had been so widely repeated that it had already taken on the status of a legend among the villagers: he had only to close his eyes for it to unfold in all its detail. It began on the gray dirt road to the fields, with his dad setting out with a throng of hard-headed peasants to sow the sorghum, a heavy wooden seed-drill across his shoulders. The road was lined with mulberry trees, their outstretched leaves as big as copper coins. Birds were chattering; the grass along the roadside was very green. The water in the ditches lay deep, patches of frogspawn shimmered on the pale yellow reeds. Dad was panting noisily under the weight of the seed-drill, when a bicycle suddenly shot out of nowhere and crashed sidelong into him. He staggered a few paces but didn't fall over, unlike the bicycle which did. Dad flung down his seed-drill, picked up the bicycle, then picked up its rider. The latter was a short-arsed individual; as soon as he tried to walk his knee joints began cracking. Dad greeted him respectfully, Officer Liu.

Officer Liu said: Have you gone blind, you dog?

Dad said: Yes, the dog is blind, don't be angry sir.

Liu: You dare to insult me? You sonofabitch bastard!

Dad: Officer, it was you who bumped into me.

Liu: Up yours!

Dad: Don't swear, sir, it was you who bumped into me.

Liu: x x x x.

Dad: You're being unreasonable, sir. Even in the old society there were honest officials who listened to reason.

Liu: What, are you saying the New Society is worse than the old society?

Dad: I never said that.

Liu: Counter-revolutionary! Renegade! I'll blow you away! Officer Liu pulled a Mauser from his waistband and pointed the gaping black muzzle at dad's chest.

Dad: I haven't done anything to deserve the death penalty.

Liu: Near as damn it you have.

Dad: Go on then, shoot me.

Liu: I didn't bring any bullets.

Dad: Fuck off then!

Liu: Maybe I can't shoot you, but there's nothing to stop me beating you up.

Officer Liu leapt at Dad like an arrow, knees cracking, and stabbed straight at the bridge of his nose with the long barrel of the pistol. Black blood began to trickle slowly from Dad's nostrils. The peasants pulled him away, and some of the older ones tried to placate Officer Liu. Officer Liu said angrily: I'll let you off this once. Dad was standing to one side, wiping away the blood with his fingers; he lifted them up and inspected them carefully. Liu said: That'll teach you some respect.

Dad: My friends, you all saw it, you'll be my witnesses — He wiped his face vigorously a couple of times, it was covered in blood — Old Liu, fuck your ancestors to the eighth generation.

As Dad stomped toward him, Old Liu raised his gun, and shouted: Come any nearer and I'll shoot! Dad said: You won't get a peep out of that gun. Dad seized Old Liu's wrist, wrested the gun away from him, and flung it viciously into the ditch, sending spray flying high into the air. Clasping Old Liu by the scruff of the neck, he shook him backward and forward for a moment, then took aim at his buttocks and gave them a gentle kick. Officer Liu plunged headfirst into the ditch, buttocks skyward; his head lodged in the sludge and his legs splashed noisily in the water. The crowd of onlookers turned pale; some edged away, others rushed down into the ditch to drag the officer out. One old man said to Dad: Quick, nephew, run for it! Dad said: Fourth uncle, we'll meet again on the road to the yellow springs [death]. And he strode off toward home.

Officer Liu was extracted by the locals, weeping and

wailing like a baby. He begged the crowd to find his gun for him, and at least a dozen of them went down into the ditch. Their searching hands stirred up plenty of mud, but they couldn't find the gun.

Dad felt among the dust on the beam and pulled down a long oil-paper sack, from which he withdrew a long, twisted gun. His eyes were glistening with tears. You mean we've still got a gun in the house? Mum asked him in astonishment. Dad said: Haven't you heard how my mum shot my dad? This was the gun she used. Mum was wide-eyed with fear. Get rid of it quick, she said. Dad said: No. Mum said: What are you going to do? Dad said: Kill someone. He now took down a powder-horn with a narrow waist, and a tin box, and deftly filled the gun with powder and shot. Dad said: Make sure that Dasuo studies hard. Make sure that he looks at this gun every day, just looks, mind, you're not to let him touch it. Have you got that? Mum said: Are you crazy? Dad pointed the gun at her: Get back!

Dad walked into the pear orchard. The blossom on the trees was like a layer of snow. He hung the gun from a tree, muzzle downward, and tied a thin piece of string to the hammer. Then he lay on his back on the ground and put the muzzle into his mouth. Eyes wide, he gazed at the golden bees and gave a sharp tug on the string. Pear blossom swirled down like snowflakes. A few bees fell to the ground, dead.

He pulled the trigger again, but still there was no report. He sat down, disheartened. The sun lay across the horizon like a doughnut, its color the same deep-fried golden brown. The pool had shrunk even smaller, the fringes of the plain grew even hazier, the white half-moon was already visible. In the distance, on a clump of reeds, insects sparkled with a green light. The ducks tucked their beaks under their wings and gazed mockingly at him. They were so close to him, getting even closer now as the sky grew darker. His stomach protested bitterly; countless roast ducks, dripping with oil, flashed before his eyes. He pulled the trigger again and again, until the percussion cap was knocked out of shape by the hammer and embedded itself inextricably in the groove. He slumped disconsolately against the hide, like an animal which had just been filleted; the sorghum stalks cracked beneath him. The wild ducks paid not the slightest heed to the noise; they were silent, motionless, a heap of dappled cobblestones. The sun disappeared, taking with it all the reds and greens, all shades of color, leaving a world returned to its original state of gray and white. The crickets and cicadas beat their wings, their chirring merging into a constant drone. On the verge of tears, he stared up at the alfalfa-colored vault of the sky, casting a sidelong glance, filled with hatred, at the gun. Was this decrepit old gun really the same one? Could such a foul-looking old wreck really have such an extraordinary history?

But when Wang Laoka started telling his tales of the old days, it really was as if they were unfolding before the villagers' eyes, and so everyone young and old loved to listen to him talking. Wang Laoka told them:

In the days of the Republic, none of the three counties controlled these parts—there were more bandits round here than hairs on a cow's back; men, women, they'd

all turn violent at the drop of a hat, they'd kill a man as
calmly as slicing a melon. Have you heard the story of
Dasuo here's granny? Well, Dasuo's grandad was a com-
pulsive gambler who lived off Dasuo's granny—that little
woman was tough, she built up a home from nothing, all
by herself, and that ain't easy for a woman. She sweated
her guts out for three years and managed to buy a few
dozen hectares of land, even a couple of horses. And what
a beauty she was, Dasuo's granny, people called her "the
queen of the eight villages." Lovely pointed bound feet
she had, a fringe like a curtain of black silk. To protect
her house and home she swapped a stone and two pecks
of grain for a gun. Now this gun had a long, long barrel
and a mahogany butt, and they say that in the dead of
night the hammer used to start clicking. She used to sling
that gun across her back and ride off into the fields on
her big horse to hunt foxes. A dead-shot she was—always
shot 'em right up the arse. But then she got sick, a terrible
thing, she was in a fever for seven whole weeks of seven
whole days. Dasuo's grandad saw his chance—off he went
roistering with whores and gambling to his heart's content: he lost all their land, even lost those two fine steeds.
When the winner came to collect the horses, Dasuo's
granny was lying on the *kang*, gasping for breath. Dasuo's
dad was just a lad of five or six then, and when he saw
that some people were trying to lead their horses away,
he yelled: Mum, someone's taking the horses! The second
she heard this, Dasuo's granny rolled straight off the *kang*,
grabbed the gun from the wall, and dragged herself pain-
fully into the courtyard. And what right have you to take
out the horses, pray? she shouted. The two fellers leading

the horses knew that this woman took no prisoners, so they said: Your man lost these horses to our boss, lady. She said: Since that's the case, might I trouble you two brothers to bring my man to see me, there's something I'd like to say to him. Dasuo's grandad—his name was Santao—was so afraid of his wife he was skulking outside the door, too scared to come in. But when he heard her shouting he knew it was too late to chicken out. He plucked up courage, did his best to look tough, marched into the courtyard, thrust out his chest and said: Hot today, isn't it? Dasuo's granny smiled and said: You lost the horses, didn't you? Santao said: Sure did. She said: So, you lost the horses, what are you going to lose next? Santao said: I'm going to lose you. She said: Good old Santao. Fate must bring enemies together, it was really my luck to marry you. You've lost my horses, lost my land, forty-nine days I've been lying here sick and you haven't so much as brought me a bowl of water. And now you think you can lose me—I reckon I'd rather lose you first. On this day next year, Santao, I'll bring the child to your grave and burn paper money for you . . . The words were hardly out of her mouth when there was a great boom; the courtyard filled with a red flash . . . and his grandad was dead. . . .

When he heard this story his dad was still alive. He asked his dad where the gun was, but his dad screamed furiously at him: You get the hell out of here!

The half-moon was becoming brighter, fireflies flitted unhurriedly, tracing a series of green-tinted arcs across his face. The pool had assumed a somber, dim, steely-gray hue, but the sky was not yet completely black—he could still make out the pale green eyes of the gold-hooped dragonflies. The chirring of the insects came in bursts, each close on the heels of the last. The damp air congealed and wafted heavenward. He wasn't watching the flock of ducks any more, he was thinking only about eating duck, again feeling the sharp contractions in his stomach. The image of the hunter with dead ducks slung all around his body became superimposed on the image of the woman warrior on horseback, her gun slung over her shoulder; at last they merged with that of the decent man under a covering of pear blossoms.

The sun had finally gone out. All that remained was a strip of fading golden warmth on the western horizon. The tip of the half-moon was rising in the south-west, scattering a tender feeling as soft as water. Mist rose from the pool like so many clumps of vegetation, the wild ducks shimmered in and out of sight through the gaps in the mist, and the splashing of big fish echoed from the water. He stood up, as if drunk or in a trance, and flexed his stiff, numb joints. He strapped on the powder-horn, slung the gun over his shoulder, and strode out of the hide. Why doesn't anything happen when I pull the trigger? He swung the gun down, cradled it in his arms, and stared at it. It shimmered with a blue glow in the moonlight. Why don't you fire? he thought. He cocked the hammer and casually pulled the trigger.

The low, rumbling explosion rolled in waves across the autumn fields and a ball of red light lit up the water-flats and the wild ducks. Shreds of iron and shards of wood hurtled through the air; the ducks took off in startled flight. He toppled slowly to the ground, trying with all his strength to open his eyes. He seemed to see the ducks floating down around him like rocks, falling onto his body, piling up into a great mound, pressing down on him so that it became difficult to breathe.

Translated by Duncan Hewitt

Hot and Cold, Measure for Measure
Wang Shuo

I

"TWO COUPLES HAVE JUST gone into 927 and 1208. Oh yeah, and there's some slut in 1713 as well"

"Right."

I put down the receiver, threw on my suit jacket, and grabbed my bag. I told Fangfang, who lay sprawled in front of the television, to get his act together. We ran downstairs and headed for the old Peugeot I'd managed to pick up for only 4,000 yuan. It was parked on the cor-

---

WANG SHUO (1958–) was the bad boy of the Chinese literary world in the 1980s and 1990s. His fiction was enormously popular, especially among young readers, because it chronicles the lives of disaffected youths during the radical transformation Chinese society experienced in the shift from a socialist to a market economy. Wang has written numerous novels, many of which have been adapted to the screen, and has also been a prolific writer of television and film scripts. Among his best-known novels are *Playing for Thrills* and *Please Don't Call Me Human*. This story, part of a larger novella, was first published in 1986. It reflects a cynical, even criminal, underworld in Beijing, one that contrasts starkly with the monumental socialist architecture of the capital city.

ner. We jumped in and took off in the direction of the Yandu Hotel, by now ablaze with lights. I found a place to park behind a row of cars in a shady street at the back of the hotel. Hopping out, we raced to catch up with a group of Japanese tourists who'd just descended from a tour bus, our ticket to the magnificent foyer that lay within.

Weining was manning the reception desk, a model of courtesy. He gave us an almost imperceptible wink. So far, so good. We went into the Gents and I pulled two police uniforms out of the bag. I handed one to Fangfang. We changed into them and took the back stairs to the ninth floor. After pausing a moment to recover our breath, we strode over to the service desk. The attendant looked up at us in surprise.

"Police. Kindly open room 927."

Picking up a set of keys, he obediently led us to a room at the end of the long corridor. Seeing the "Do Not Disturb" sign, he turned and said, "But the guest is in the room."

"We know. Open it."

He did as he was told and stood to one side.

"Now get out of here," Fangfang said with a dismissive wave of the hand. As soon as the attendant disappeared down the corridor, we stormed into the room.

We left with Yahong in tow and several thousand yuan in crisp new bills in the bag. Our expressions were deadly serious when we passed the attendant, but as soon as we entered the lift Fangfang and Yahong burst out laughing.

"What's so goddamn funny?" I said, then started laughing myself.

"Wait for us in the bar downstairs," I told Yahong. "We

still have a guy on the twelfth floor to deal with." We dropped Yahong off on the ground floor and took the lift back up.

Fifteen minutes later we were back in our street clothes and in the bar with Yahong and the other tart. We had a drink together and Fangfang left with Yahong on his arm. I gave Weining a call at the desk to let him know the job was done. As for the hooker on the seventeenth floor, I told him to let her have a good night's sleep. He could call the police the next morning. I left the hotel in a calm mood, arm in arm with the other girl. By this stage Fangfang had already brought the car around; we hopped in and sped off.

I was woken the next morning by the telephone. Yahong, who lay sleeping by my side, answered it and said it was Weining. He'd called to say that the two suckers had left that morning after paying the bill, while the other girl had been picked up by the police as she left. Yahong rolled over and went back to sleep. I lay there chain-smoking. Sunlight streamed in through the heavy curtains. I crept over to the window to gaze out through the narrow crack at the bright and busy street below. I drew the curtains shut. I hate sunny mornings; the sight of all those people happily toddling off to work and school makes me feel lonely. I've nothing to do in the daytime; no business to conduct and no one to see. All my friends are asleep. I smoked another five cigarettes, then checked the date on the calendar before finally throwing on some clothes and having a quick wash. I left the apartment building and walked to the bus stop, passing my car, which I'd left parked at the corner. It was past rush hour, but the passengers were still packed in like sardines. A middle-aged man had just got off the bus and I was about to grab his seat when I saw a young woman with a child in her arms. I gave her my seat.

"Thank you." Smiling, she turned to her child. "Say, 'Thank you, Uncle.'"

"Thank you, Uncle," the child obliged, and I smiled back at him. Reaching into his pocket, he extracted a bar of chocolate in a brightly colored wrapper. He tore off the paper and was at the point of putting it into his mouth when he noticed I was watching him. He held it up to me.

"No, thanks. Uncle doesn't want any."

"Go on, it's okay."

"No, really. Uncle's got to get off the bus now."

I squeezed off the bus. From there I made my way to the clinic attached to my work unit and asked for the sick leave form in triplicate. Then I phoned a buddy of mine who has liver problems and asked him to go take my blood test for me. My next stop was the business district, where I deposited last night's earnings in accounts at two different banks. Both accounts are in the names of my late parents. My final call was at the post office, where I remitted the registration fee and a year's tuition to a correspondence school. It's the type of school where you can pick up a university degree without ever taking an exam. I'd chosen law for my major.

Having completed the day's tasks, I went to lunch at an upmarket but quiet restaurant. The food at this place is tops. I started getting into the red wine, picking a bottle for its pretty label, and rounded the meal off with an ice cream sundae drenched in chocolate syrup. I didn't leave till well into the afternoon. At the newsstand I bought the morning and evening papers, then went to the Telephone and Telegraph Building. There I grabbed a seat in the waiting room for long-distance calls and read the papers at a leisurely pace. At dusk I called home and spoke to Fangfang. He'd spent the day playing chess with Weining, who'd been there since morning. By now Fangfang had won four games, drawn three, and lost five. They were planning a mah-jongg session for the evening. I told him I'd be home late and hung up.

It was late spring. Everywhere the trees and grass provided a dense green cover and the flowers were in full bloom. An evening concert was being held in the park, so I stood in front of the box office waiting for someone to return a ticket. Eventually some old guy gave me his, but there was a couple with only one ticket so I gave it to them, refusing their offer to pay double for it.

I wandered along a long causeway with tall pillars the paint of which had grown dry and was crusty and peeling. It was then that I saw this attractive young girl sitting on a white marble platform, reading. She sat there with her legs crossed and dangling, swinging back and forth over the side. She held her book in one hand while the other was engaged in extracting melon seeds from a small bag by her side. The discarded shells had been placed in a tidy pile. She sat there softly humming, turning a page from time to time. She seemed so laid-back, she looked cool. I stole up behind her and tried to see what book could be so engrossing. I skimmed the page over her shoulder—it was a heavy, abstract tome on literary theory, too dull for words. I was at the point of walking away when I heard her say, "Over your head?" She was grinning at me.

I felt myself blushing. I didn't know I could still blush. Amazing. Getting a hold of myself, I responded, "Right, so you're a student. But isn't this business of reading in the park at night a bit of a put-on?"

"Actually, I've been here all afternoon. Look how much I've read!"

I flicked through the pages she'd said she'd read. Impressive. But considering the subject matter, I was dubious, so I asked, "How can you possibly read this so quickly?"

"Because I don't understand it either, that's why."

We laughed.

"I'm not going to read any more tonight," she put the book down.

"What are you up to?"

"Nothing."

"Stay and talk for a bit, then."

"Sure." I sat down beside her. She gave me a handful of melon seeds. I've never been able to crack them open with my teeth, they sort of just disintegrate in my mouth.

"Here. I'll show you." She demonstrated how to crack a seed with your teeth, her white teeth gleaming as she did so. Somewhat self consciously, I closed my mouth to hide my nicotine teeth. She didn't seem to notice, gazing around as she swung her legs.

"Which university are you at?" I'd noticed the university badge on her sweater.

"I suppose this is your pickup line. Then you'll tell me

where you study, how close our campuses are, and how easy it would be to see a lot of each other . . ."

"Do I look like a student?" was my reply. "I'm an ex-con from a labor camp. At the moment I'm trying my hand at blackmail."

"I don't give a damn what you are." She smiled down at her toes as if they were terribly amusing. "I really couldn't care less."

We sat there in silence for what seemed an eternity, gazing contentedly at the setting sun and the rapidly approaching darkness. The clouds were still visible and quite magnificent.

"Look, that cloud looks like Marx, and that one over there looks a bit like a pirate, don't you think?"

"How old are you?"

She turned and studied me. "You haven't had much experience with women, have you?"

"No, I haven't." I delivered this line totally poker-faced.

"I knew it the moment I saw you. You're just a kid. I could tell from the way you hovered there in the distance, trying to pluck up the courage to come over and talk to me. You were afraid I was going to say something to embarrass you, weren't you?"

"Actually, I've slept with more than a hundred girls."

She shrieked with laughter.

"You have a moronic laugh," I told her.

She stopped laughing and threw me a resentful look. "Look, I'm not dumping on you, so lay off me, okay? To tell you the truth, I've been going out with someone for over a year." She smiled smugly.

"Who is he? Some fuckwit classmate of yours?"

"He's definitely no fuckwit! He's a cadre in the Student Union!"

"Doesn't that prove my point? You can't get much worse than that."

"Hmph. You should talk. Your mother is the only woman who's ever kissed you, that's for sure."

"If I were him, at least I'd be man enough to sleep with you," I said with a smirk. "Tell me, does he?" Although it was already dark, I could see she had turned bright red.

"He respects me!"

I sniggered. "Respect? Bullshit! Give me a break. You don't really think I was born yesterday, do you?"

This got her. She sat there for ages without a word. I whistled to myself. Then I pulled out a pack of cigarettes, put one into my mouth, and offered one to her. She shook her head.

"So that's it? You'll read in a park, but you don't smoke. You're not really as trendy as you look."

"Cut the crap." She wasn't one to accept defeat. "Give me one."

I gave her the one from my lips. She took one puff and started coughing. I put my arm around her shoulders, and although she trembled, she didn't object. I drew her toward me and she examined me closely. Then she threw off my arm and burst out laughing.

"I'm beginning to believe this business about the hundred girls."

"Hey, it's the gospel truth. You know what they call me? 'Shotgun.'"

She gathered up her books. My laughter had a malicious tinge. "I've frightened you."

"No, you haven't." She stood up. "But . . . I've got to be going."

"How about a little name and address action before you go?"

Her eyes flashed, and she hopped off the platform. "So! At first I really did think you were different from the rest. But you're as crass as they come."

"Okay, so I'm crass. I'm not going to hold you up if you want to go. But," I called out to her as she walked away, "if we meet again we're friends, right?"

"Sure." She walked away laughing.

I sat there grinning to myself for a while, then I split, too.

11

Fangfang and I were cruising down one of the main drags, keeping an eye out for the talent. When we found any, Fangfang would pull up alongside the curb and we'd try to chat her up. If she wouldn't take the bait, we'd just laugh and drive on, taking the piss out of her as we went. Suddenly we spotted two young women who'd just come out of a grocery store with some fruit juice, and they were laughing and talking as they strolled along. Fangfang pulled up beside them. Winding down the window, I called out "Hey!" The two girls stopped and turned around.

"Don't you recognize me?" I asked.

"Oh, it's you!" replied one of the girls, grinning. "What a coincidence. What're you doing?"

"Looking for you," I said. "I haven't stopped thinking about you since we met."

"Ha! What a come-on!"

"Do you know him?" the second girl whispered to her friend.

"No, not really," the girl I'd met in the park told her friend, "but he admits himself that he's a real *liumang*."

We all laughed at this. Leaning across, I opened the back door. "Jump in, we'll take you for a spin." As the two girls climbed in, Fangfang put the car into gear and we took off.

"Oh, by the way, I'm Zhang Ming, and this is my friend Fangfang."

Fangfang turned around and smiled.

It was my girl's turn. "This is my friend Chen Weiling, and I'm Wu Di,'"

"Di? Oh, right, that means 'terrific.'"

"Yeah." Wu Di nodded, smiling.

"Where are you headed?"

"To the auditorium just around the corner."

"What's the movie?" Fangfang kept his eyes on the road.

"Oh, it's not a movie. It's a lecture: 'Young Readers Discuss Spiritual Civilization.'"

"What the hell is that?"

"It's probably one of those student things." Fangfang pulled a face.

"You're studying arts subjects, aren't you?"

"How did you know?" Wu Di asked with curious delight.

"It's simple. Women who study science look like the back end of a bus."

"You're outrageous." She laughed uncontrollably, obviously pleased by the flattery. "We study English."

"And what are you? Taxi drivers?" Chen Weiling asked with all the warmth of an iceberg.

"I've already told Wu Di. We're two ex-cons from a labor reform camp."

Wu Di just smiled, but Chen Weiling frowned and gazed out the window. It was obvious she didn't believe me. She'd already decided we were nothing but a couple of bored playboys, beneath contempt. "He told me," Wu Di addressed her friend while looking straight at me, "that he's slept his way through the phone book."

Chen Weiling glared at me briefly. To say she didn't like me would be an understatement. She wasn't a bit like Wu Di. I couldn't really give a fuck what she thought. She didn't even vaguely interest me.

We managed to park right outside the auditorium. A great many students were milling around in groups of three and four, people were rushing to and fro. A real lively scene.

I motioned to Wu Di to come closer and whispered in her ear, "Meet me at the Monument to the People's Heroes tomorrow at four, okay?"

She smiled. Meanwhile, Fangfang was attempting to hold a conversation with Chen Weiling. She'd already rendered him completely speechless.

"Are you frightened your boyfriend will be jealous?"

"He doesn't care who I see. He's very open-minded."

"Then what are you frightened of?"

"Come in and listen to the speeches, and I'll tell you afterward whether I'm coming or not."

"I really can't bear the thought of listening to those wankers. Anyway, why bother listening to them when you've got me?"

"If you don't come, then tomorrow's definitely off."

"Hey, Fangfang, what do you think, shall we go in or not?"

"If we're going, let's go." Fangfang sounded completely indifferent.

"Anyway, we've got nothing else on, so we might as well check it out."

"Okay, let's go." I turned to Wu Di. "You'd better come tomorrow."

"We'll talk about it later."

As she got out of the car, Chen Weiling asked Wu Di, "Where'd he ask you to go?"

"Nowhere in particular. He just asked me to go out with him, that's all."

"And you're going?" Chen Weiling's tone of voice was severe.

"I didn't say either way." Wu Di was deliberately vague.

Fangfang and I got out of the car and followed the two girls inside. They ran into some classmates and stopped to chat, so the two of us went on ahead and found some empty seats on the aisle. Soon they came looking for us. I tossed aside the bookbags on the two seats next to us, at which point the girl who'd been saving the seats for her friends mumbled something and threw me an angry look. When Wu Di settled herself, she proceeded to give a preview of what was to come, sort of a vaccination. She told us how good the speakers were, how what they had to say was jam-packed with educational value, truly earth-shattering stuff, and that you could never get bored no matter how many times you heard it.

The first speaker was a woman worker of some description. As soon as she took the stage Fangfang and I burst out laughing. The speakers ran the usual spectrum of workers, peasants, students, and businessmen. They all spoke very forcefully, dramatically waving their hands about and shouting so loudly that the veins in their necks and faces bulged. As for content, it was all the standard bullshit about how young people should study hard and love the motherland and such. I'd heard it all a million times before. They threw in all the usual historical anecdotes, so it sounded like a recitation from the *Popular Household Book of Historical Facts*. Then they recited a few poems of the "rabidly revolutionary" school. It was like all these people had popped out of the same boring mold. When some slick young man took the stage and started rabbiting on about how the young people of today should "cultivate the flowers of love," I laughed so hard I almost wet my pants. This was so different from the appreciative murmurs issuing from the rest of the audience that Chen Weiling glared at me angrily. Wu Di gave me a small but sharp nudge.

"You should pay a bit more attention." Chen Weiling was pissed off. "Someone as ignorant as you could do with a little education."

I replied in my best embarrassingly loud voice: "I was getting this sort of education when you were still a twinkle in your daddy's eye."

Chen Weiling turned bright red. Wu Di, at a loss for what else to do and wanting to avoid the burning looks coming from all directions, pretended to be totally absorbed by the lecture.

"Just look at you!" Fangfang said to Chen Weiling. "All this fuckin' education and you've still got shit for brains. What a joke." He turned to me. "Come on, don't waste your breath. We're outta here."

We went out into the foyer and stood there smoking, laughing about the whole thing, when Fangfang suddenly nudged me. "Hey." I turned around and saw Wu Di coming in. She caught sight of us and approached somewhat timidly, her face reddening.

"Are you angry with us?"

"No. Should I be?"

"That classmate of yours is bloody rude," Fangfang commented.

Looking up at me, Wu Di said, "You really insulted her. Right now she's sitting there crying, you know."

"Well, say sorry for us, will you? We didn't mean to upset her. She a good friend of yours?" I added.

"Sort of. We're classmates, but I wouldn't say we're the greatest of friends."

"Wu Di!"

"Yeah?" Wu Di spun around to see the young student who'd just been speaking walking toward us.

"This is my friend," was her muttered introduction. She blushed when she saw the look of amusement in our eyes.

"Oh, so you're Wu Di's friends." He sounded quite enthusiastic. "My speech must have been really awful to make you laugh like that."

"Oh, no, no, no. It was really good," I said in my most courteous voice.

"A lot better than the others." Even Fangfang felt sorry for him.

"I was told to do it, and I hardly had any time to prepare, so—" He was a down-to-earth sort of guy.

"Han Jin!" By now the foyer was crammed with people and a group of guys were calling to Wu Di's boyfriend.

"Catch you later," said Han Jin, moving off to join them.

"Nice guy," I remarked appreciatively.

"I can tell you don't think much of him." Wu Di looked deeply distressed.

"What do you mean? We were just being assholes, don't take it so seriously! We're just working-class guys, about as low as they come," I said in all sincerity. "We wouldn't dare look down on anyone."

"Forget it, no need to put yourself down." Wu Di's sidelong glance showed her growing annoyance.

"Mr. Shi!" she suddenly called out to a man about thirty years of age.

"Oh, hello, Wu Di." The man stopped and chatted happily with Wu Di until he caught sight of Fangfang and me. His smile evaporated.

"Hello, *Mister* Shi," Fangfang addressed him with obvious sarcasm.

"Hello Zhang Ming, Fangfang." Shi Yide smiled unconvincingly. We all shook hands.

"A university cadre, are you? Will wonders never cease?" I kidded him. "A real Youth League cadre. Well, where there's a will there's a way." Then I explained to Wu Di, who was standing there really out of it, "We're old classmates. None of us ever graduated. He ended up working for the school's Youth League, while the two of us were expelled."

III

I sat on the stone steps of the Monument to the People's Heroes. I didn't know if she'd come. It didn't worry me—it was a lovely day and a warm wind was caressing me. A crowd of old folks and children were flying kites on Tiananmen Square. Phoenixes pranced, eagles soared, and swallows fluttered against the blue sky. But everyone, foreign tourists as well as the Chinese, was watching a brightly colored centipede over ten meters long that this old guy was flying. It was rising and falling in a leisurely, relaxed way, and the crowd was staring up at it, clapping and shouting.

Over to the west side of the square, in front of the Great Hall of the People, the premier was conducting a formal welcoming ceremony for some foreign dignitary. As the cannon was fired in salute, the immaculate army band played the two national anthems on their gleaming brass instruments. The two heads of state, accompanied by their retinues, strode along a red carpet, reviewing the combined services' guard of honor.

I looked at my watch. It was past four. I stood up and climbed to the base of the monument to look out over the square. In the distance I saw a girl in a cream-colored embroidered silk blouse and a short blue and white batik skirt running in my direction. She slowed down only when she reached the flower garden in front of the monument. She looked around. Her gaze passed over me, but I didn't call out to her. I watched patiently as she checked the time on her watch and moved the minute hand back. Slowly she ambled up the steps of the monument and over to where I was standing—and stopped abruptly. I burst out laughing. "I wanted to see if you could spot me or not. Am I that inconspicuous?"

She just laughed and looked at me without saying anything.

"You're ten minutes late."

"No, I'm not!" She raised her slender wrist to show me her watch.

"Give me a break." I had caught her little game. "I saw you move the watch hand."

She giggled with embarrassment. The guard of honor presented arms as the two heads of state watched solemnly from the reviewing stand.

"I didn't think you'd show."

"Why not?"

"I thought Shi Yide and Chen Weiling were bound to say all sorts of bad things about me."

She laughed and glanced at me: "Shi Yide didn't really put you down. He said that although you and he didn't hit it off very well then, he always thought you were a really clever person, just a bit self-destructive."

"And what did Chen Weiling say?"

She smiled.

"Go on."

"It's not nice."

"Oh, come on. What do I care what people say about me?"

"She said you were a shameless *liumang*, the dregs of society. But really, you did treat her awfully badly."

"Did she tell you not to have anything more to do with me?"

"Yes."

"But you came all the same."

"Well, who's she to tell me what to do?"

"Right on."

"Of course."

The ceremony in front of the Great Hall was over. The motorcade of black luxury sedans drove off in single file behind a police motorcycle escort. The spectators slowly dispersed.

Wu Di and I walked along Qianmen East Street toward Chongwenmen. To begin with, we walked slightly apart from each other, but there were so many people and vehicles about that we were either always being separated or we kept bumping into each other. So it was quite natural for her to take my arm. I didn't have any job planned for that evening, so I could spend it with her. To tell the truth, the only thing I had in mind was getting her into the sack.

Yesterday in the car, after the lecture, I'd said to Fang-fang: "I can't stand that bitch. She's about as warm as a piece of cloisonné."

"Who? Chen Weiling?"

"Of course. Our little Wu Di isn't bad, though, is she?"

"Have you scored a date?"

"*Mais oui!*"

"Hey, foreigner, you'll go far."

"She's really quite cute. But a little too naive for my taste. I don't feel right about putting the make on her."

"Don't make me barf. As if it'll be the first time she's

done it." Fangfang put his foot down on the accelerator and turned a corner sharply.

"No way. She's an innocent. Hit the books all during high school and then went straight to university." I recited the curriculum vitae as I smoked a cigarette. "It's all a novelty for her. She wants to try everything. She's at the age where she's attracted to danger, she'd run straight at the barrel of a gun. Give me the key to your apartment, will you?"

"I should warn you, I'm a dangerous friend to have. I get up to things you don't even know about."

We were having a meal at a very quiet restaurant. After the waiters served the meal, they retreated to a far corner. I know that the best way of chatting up a girl who despises everything conventional and fancies herself a nonconformist is to make yourself out to be a bastard. Not only will she think you're more interesting, she'll even like you better for it. It's just like if you describe someone being really hideous when in fact they're not that ugly. A girl will then try to find your good points rather than being hypercritical and just look for faults.

"I'm greedy, a sex maniac, and a complete moral wipeout. Every day I dress up as a police officer in order to blackmail Hong Kong businessmen and foreigners. I'm a criminal at large. You'd be doing everyone a service if you reported me to the police."

"I could tell right from the beginning. I'm actually an undercover police officer, and I've got you under surveillance."

"You've got a tape recorder in your handbag, right?"

"You bet."

"Is that guy over there one of yours?" I pointed to a waiter standing at attention with his hands at his side, staring across from the other side of the room.

"Yes." Wu Di looked across at the waiter and then back at me. She laughed. "Our men are everywhere."

We had a good laugh and then chatted about other things.

"Did you think the lectures yesterday were really that unbearable?" Wu Di asked.

"Oh, they weren't that bad." I drank some wine. "To be able to go on and on about obvious things like that is a kind of talent in itself."

"You looked as if you totally despised the lot of us."

"I just felt that it was all a bit beneath you university students to like that kind of thing. If you want to find out about something, why don't you just read a few books? I got so fed up with the patronizing tone of those speakers. What do they take you for? Who's more stupid than whom around here? All this crap about how to study, even how to fall in love. It's none of their bloody business. They're all still wet behind the ears, but they're up there preaching at others."

"Does that mean Your Majesty reads and searches for the truth on his own?"

"Wrong!" I grinned at her cheekily. "I'm not the type of person to get anything out of books. Why not live the way you want to? Enjoy yourself, go through a few hard times, cry a bit, laugh a bit, do what moves you. Better than burying yourself in a book and heaving sighs over someone else's life. You have to take control of your own life."

"But can't you learn from other people's experience and mistakes? Doesn't it help you to define your own aims more clearly?"

"I don't want to know how things are going to end up. Slogging along at something, bit by bit, step by step, that's too boring. The more vision, the less excitement. If I knew my next move and what I'd be up against each step of the way and what would happen each time, I'd immediately lose all interest in living."

"And so . . . ?"

"And so, as soon as I discovered that I'd earn only 56 yuan a month after graduation from university, I left school. And so, as soon as I discovered I was going to be a lowly clerk all my life, I stopped going to work."

"But you can't avoid death. . . ."

"So I don't waste my time. Eat, drink, and rage to the limit. As long as you have to live, you might as well try everything, right? Stick your chopsticks into every dish at the banquet."

"Aren't the hundred 'dishes' you've tasted enough for you? You can die happy!"

"Each is different. Even noodles can be the stuff of banquets. I mean, there's always something new to experience. For instance, a week ago, I never dreamed I'd meet you. And now, here we are having dinner together, an intimate tête-à-tête. Who knows where things will go from here? Could be quite exciting, couldn't it? It all depends on us. Don't you think this is fun, what life's all about?"

"Tell me," said Wu Di curiously. "What do you think could happen between us?"

"It's possible you'll fall in love with me." She was

hooked. I was delighted. "And I might fall in love with you."

"But I already have a boyfriend."

"So what! Perhaps this boyfriend, this Han Jin, will turn into the person you most detest. Perhaps you'll even die at his hands. When you read a book, you flick over the first few pages and you know what's going to happen next. But life is revealed one step at a time. You can't even tell whether it's going to turn out as a comedy or a tragedy. Do you like sad movies or comedies?"

"Sad films! I love films that make me cry, they're the best."

"I'll definitely make you cry."

"Do you want to hurt me?"

"It depends what you mean by hurt. If, for instance, you fall in love with me and if, well . . ."

Wu Di smiled, nodding her head. "Go on."

". . . you fall in love with me, and after we finish dinner, you go home with me. I fall in love with you too—it's not impossible—let's say I fall deeply in love with you. Hey, don't laugh. But you're a fickle kind of girl and you fall in love with someone else. I'm grief-stricken, but, nobly, I let you go. Years pass by. We grow old. We meet again by chance in this restaurant. I'm all alone in this world. You're also unhappy in your old age. You feel sentimental about times past. You cry."

Wu Di laughed so hard she had to spit the mouthful of wine she had just drunk back into the glass. Opening her red, moist lips, she said, "It doesn't sound to me as if you don't read any books. It sounds to me as if you've read too many bad romances."

"Well, don't you think it's a possibility?"

"No way. The only possible scenario would be like this: I fall in love with you, but you don't love me at all. I die for you. You—"

"It sounds as if both of us could be novelists."

"It's always the man who's at fault."

"Okay. Let's see what happens next. The essential thing is to get this story moving. Now, Chapter One: I've already fallen in love with you."

"But I haven't fallen in love with you." Wu Di laughed and, blushing, looked straight into my amorous eyes.

When the waiter came with the bill, Wu Di insisted on paying. In order to preserve her dignity and to make this scheme of mine seem more innocent, I let her do as she wanted.

It was already dark outside. The streets were still crowded and the traffic quite heavy. But when Wu Di took my arm again, I knew I had succeeded. This wasn't just a technical maneuver, the normal response to walking in a crowd of people, but the touch of a lover, shy, bashful, and clinging.

Traditional morality being held in universal disdain these days, I didn't have to make much effort to help her shed the slight residual sense of responsibility she felt toward Han Jin.

Fangfang's apartment was the usual thing: thin walls and hot, stuffy rooms. It was very easy getting her to take her clothes off. So as to give her a bit more courage, I left the lights off. She really was quite cool and composed about the whole thing. Actually, when kissing her, I even thought she seemed quite experienced. Of course she told me it was her "first time" and I said it was my "first time" too. Afterward, she wept in silence. I didn't hear anything. The room was pitch-black, and I couldn't see anything either. But I could tell something was wrong. She hadn't lied to me after all. I touched her face; it was soaked in tears.

"It really was your first time?"

She didn't say anything. I felt a little alarmed. I knew what the first time would mean to her. Things didn't look too good for the future. She could make things complicated. I didn't love her. I didn't love anyone. "Love" is such a ridiculous word. Although I often use it, I say it in the same easy way I do a word like "shit."

I woke up feeling very groggy the next morning. I looked up at the girl sitting next to me. I didn't feel a thing for her. She hadn't slept all night. Her hair was all tousled and she leaned over, looking at me with her bright, teary eyes and kissing me.

"You're awake." She smiled at me, an ingratiating and self-deprecating smile.

I shut my eyes. My dissipated and irregular life-style had wrought havoc with my health. I felt weak and clapped-out. I didn't even feel up to giving her a smile in return. Anyway, there was no need for me to try to please her anymore.

"Do you love me?" she whispered as she stroked my face.

"Yeah." I was thinking of how I could get rid of her.

"I love you too, really. You don't know how much I love you."

"I know."

"Shall we get married?"

I chuckled a little, not wanting to dampen her spirits.

"The two of us'll be so happy," she daydreamed excitedly as she cuddled up to me. "I'll be really good to you, make you really comfortable. We'll never quarrel, never get cross with each other. Everyone'll be envious of us. Do you want a boy or a girl?"

"A neuter."

"You're horrible! Don't go back to sleep, I won't let you!"

I opened my eyes. "I'm really tired, okay?" I leaned over and looked at my watch on the table. "You should get going to class."

"I'm not going."

"Hey, come on. You really ought to go, it's not right for you to skip class."

"I don't want to go. I want to stay here and look at you."

"You'll see plenty of me soon enough. Now I just want to sleep. . . . Hey, what's wrong?"

She was biting her lip, and her eyes were filling with tears. She didn't say anything.

"Okay, okay." I patted her cheek. "Now you must go to class. I'll call you this afternoon. Don't be cross. I'm only thinking of you."

I brushed my lips against hers, and she looked a bit happier. She put her arms around me and kissed me. Then she got up and put her clothes on.

"Will you see me off?" She had dressed and was standing at the mirror tying up her hair with a rubber band.

"Listen, the neighbors are a bit of a nuisance," I said,

a bit fed up by now. "If they see the two of us together, they're bound to talk."

"All right. I don't need you to see me out. What time will you call me this afternoon?"

"When I get up."

"Make it as soon as you can."

She walked over, cupped my face in her hands, and kissed me hard and long. I almost passed our from lack of oxygen.

"See you!" She left, radiant with joy.

"See you."

I stared stupidly around me for a few minutes and then turned over and went back to sleep.

Wu Di falls in love with Zhang Ming but becomes deeply disillusioned. She ends up a prostitute and commits suicide when their gang is busted by the police. Zhang Ming is sentenced again to labor reform camp. When he's released, he meets a girl who reminds him very much of Wu Di. . . .

Wu Di, the slightly rebellious student seeking personal liberation, might, if she had lived, just as easily have joined the Protest Movement as been seduced by Wang's "hero."

Translated by Brigette Holland (with Jonathan Hutt)

Man of La Mancha

Chu T'ien-hsin

STRICTLY SPEAKING, that was the day I began thinking about making preparations for my own death.

I should probably start from the night before.

Because a short essay of absolutely no importance was
due the following noon, my brain, as usual, defied orders
and turned itself on, ignoring the lure of the dream world
and causing me to stay awake till dawn.

A few hours later, barely making it there before break-

CHU T'IEN-HSIN (1958–) and her sister, Chu T'ien-wen, are
among the best-known women writers in contemporary Taiwan.
Both began their careers in the 1970s writing fiction that expresses
sentimental and nostalgic longings for the lost homeland (the
mainland, from which their father, himself a well-known writer,
had fled in the late 1940s). Her most recent fiction, particular the
stories in *Ancient Capital* (1997), from which this piece comes,
is much more stylistically experimental and is centered on difficult issues of personal and cultural memory. Without linear
plots, the stories in *Ancient Capital* are concerned primarily with
the complex history, memory, and cultural makeup of Taipei, a
city occupied at various times by the Dutch, the Manchus, the
Japanese, and finally the Nationalists. Though this history is not
dealt with explicitly in the story, it lurks beneath the surface of
the protagonist's personal identity crisis.

fast hours ended, I set to work in a Japanese-style chain coffee shop, effortlessly finishing that short, unimportant essay. It was then that I had the leisure to notice that, in order to fortify myself against the cold blasts from the air conditioner, I'd already downed five or six scalding refills of coffee, which had turned my fingers and toes numb, as if I'd been poisoned. I quietly stretched in my cramped seat, only to discover that my lips were so numb I couldn't open them to yawn. Even more strange was that my internal organs, whose existence had pretty much gone unnoticed over the three decades or so they'd been with me, were now frozen and shrunken, like little clenched fists, hanging tightly in their places inside me. I looked up at the girl who, in her clean, crisply pressed, nurselike uniform and apron, diligently refilled my cup over and over, and just about called out to her for help.

I was anxiously pondering the language to use in seeking help from a stranger—even though this stranger was all smiles and would never refuse requests such as "Please give me another pat of butter," "Let me have another look at the menu," "Where can I make a phone call?" etc. But, "Help me?" "Please call me an ambulance?" "Please help me stand up?". . .

Yet for someone else, obviously, it was too late. The noontime headline news over the coffee shop radio announced that a certain second-generation descendant of the *ancient régime* had been discovered early that morning dead in a hospital examination room, still in the prime of his youth, cause of death unknown, a peaceful look on his face. Which meant he hadn't even had time to struggle or call out for help.

That was all I needed: picking up my essay and bag, I paid and left.

I refused to pass out during the few minutes I spent waiting for a bus or a taxi (whichever came first), but if I'd wanted to, I could have slumped to the pavement and plunged into a deep slumber. Then a series of screams would have erupted around me, mixed with whisperings, and many heads, framed in the light behind them, would have bent down and appeared on the retina of my enlarged iris, as in the camera shot used in all movies for such scenes.

No matter how you looked at it, it would have been a pretty loutish way to go, so I refused to fall or even to rest, though by then the chill from my internal organs was spreading out to my flesh and skin. I forced myself to head toward an old and small nearby clinic. My mind was a blank; I have no idea how long it took me to get there. "I'm going to faint, please help me," I said to the work-study student nurse, who was about the same age as the coffee shop girl who'd served me.

When I came to, I was lying on a narrow examination bed; the gray-haired old doctor, mixing Mandarin and Taiwanese, answered the puzzled look and questions brimming in my eyes with a voice that seemed very loud, very far away, and very slow: "Not enough oxygen to your heart. We're giving you an IV. Lie here a while before you leave. The nurse can help you phone your family, if you want. Don't stay up too late or eat anything that might upset you. Arrhythmia is a serious matter."

With that warning, he went off to see the next patient.

So concise, so precise, he'd pinpointed my problems: insomnia, too much coffee, and arrhythmia. Strange, why was a very, very cold tear hanging in the corner of each of my eyes?

I still felt cold, but it was only the chill of the old Japanese-style clinic, no longer the deadly silent, numbing cold from the gradual loss of vital signs I'd experienced a few minutes earlier. But I hesitated, like a spirit floating in the air, as if I could choose not to return to my body. I missed the body that had nearly slumped to the pavement a few minutes before. The site of the near fall was the bus stop in front of McDonald's, so there would have been young mothers with their children and old men with grandchildren waiting for the bus. The sharp-eyed youngsters would be the first to spot it, then the mothers would vigilantly pull them away or draw them under their wings for protection, instinctively believing that it must be a beggar, a vagrant, or a mental patient, or maybe someone suffering from the effects of the plague, cholera, or epilepsy. But some of the grandpas who'd seen more of the world would come up to check and then, judging from my more or less respectable attire, take me off the list of the aforementioned suspects and decide to save me.

Looking into my wide-open but enlarged irises, they'd shout, "Who are you? Who should we call? What's the number?" They'd also order one of the gawking young women, "Go call an ambulance."

Who am I? Who should I call? What number?

I'd think back to how, on busy mornings, my significant other would lay out his schedule for the day, and I'd promptly forget; it would go something like this: "At ten-thirty I'm going to X's office; at noon I have to be at XX Bank as a guarantor. Do we have bills to pay? In the afternoon I'll go. . . . Want me to get you. . . . Or page me when you decide. . . . "

So I'd give up searching for and trying to recall his whereabouts.

Grandpa would say, "We have no choice, we have to go through his bag."

And, under watchful eyes, so as to avoid suspicion, he'd open my bag. Let's see, plenty of money—coins and bills—some ATM receipts, one or two unused lengths of dental floss, a claim ticket for film developing and a coupon for a free enlargement from the same photo studio; here, here's a business card . . . given to me yesterday by a friend, for a super-cheap London B&B (16 pounds a night), at 45 Lupton Street, phone and fax (071) 4854075. Even though it would have an address and a phone number, it would of course provide no clue to my identity. So Grandpa would have to check my pockets; in one he'd find a small packet of facial tissues, in the other, after ordering the onlookers to help turn me over, a small stack of napkins with the name of the Japanese coffee shop I'd just visited printed in the comer. Different from the plain, unprinted McDonald's napkins in their pockets.

Then someone would take out that short, insignificant essay and start to read, but be unable to retrieve, from my insignificant pen name, any information to decipher my identity.

Finally a tender-hearted, timid young mother would cover her sobbing face and cry out, "Please, someone hurry, send him to the hospital."

That's what scared me most. Just like that, I could become a nameless vegetable lying in a hospital for who knows how long; of course, even more likely, I'd become an anonymous corpse picked up on a sidewalk and lie for years in cold storage at the city morgue.

Could all this really result from an absence of identifiable items?

From that moment on, from that very moment on, I began to think about making preparations for my own death—or should I say, it occurred to me that I ought to prepare for unpredictable, unpreventable circumstances surrounding my death?

Maybe you'll say nothing could be easier, all I had to do was start carrying a picture ID or a business card, like someone with a heart condition who's never without a note that says: whoever finds this please send the bearer to a certain hospital, phone the following family members, in the order their numbers appear here, and, most important, take a glycerin pill out of the little bottle in my pocket and place it under my tongue. But no, that's not what I meant. Maybe I should say that was the genesis of my worries but, as my thoughts unfolded, they went far beyond that.

Let me cite a couple of examples by way of explanation.

Not long ago I found a wallet in a phone booth. It was a poor-quality knock-off of a name-brand item. So I opened it without much curiosity, with the simple intention of finding the owner's address in order to, as my good deed for the day, mail it back to him or her—before opening it, I couldn't get a sense of the owner's gender, given its unisex look.

The wallet was quite thick, even though the money

inside amounted to a meager 400 NT. In addition to a color photo of Amy Lau, it was all puffed up with over a dozen cards: a phone card, a KTV member discount card, a student card from a chain hair salon, a point-collecting card from a bakery, a raffle ticket stub, a membership exchange card for a TV video game club, an iced tea shop manager's business card, an honor card for nonsmokers, etc.

I probably didn't look beyond the third card before I was confident I could describe the wallet's owner; a sixteen-or seventeen-year-old insipid (in my view) female student. That, in fact, turned out to be the case; my assumption was corroborated by a swimming pool membership card, which included her school and grade, so I could return the wallet to her when I found the time.

Here's another example. I don't know if you've read the autobiography of the Spanish director, Luis Buñuel, but I recall that he said he stopped going on long trips after turning sixty because he was afraid of dying in a foreign land, afraid of the movielike scene of opened suitcases and documents strewn all over the ground, ambulance sirens and flashing police lights, hotel owners, local policemen, small-town reporters, gawkers, total chaos, awkward and embarrassing. Most important, he was probably afraid that, lacking the ability to defend himself, he'd be identified and labeled, whether or not he'd led a life that was serious, complex, worthy.

Here's another related example, although it doesn't concern death, taken from a certain short story that nicely describes the extramarital affair of a graceful and refined lady. When, by chance, she encounters her lover, and sex is on the agenda, she changes her mind. What stops her is surely not morality, nor her loving husband, who treats her just fine, nor the enjoyment-killing idea that there's no time for birth control measures. Rather, it's that she left home that day on the spur of the moment to take a stroll and do some shopping during a time when everything was scarce, and she was wearing ordinary cotton under-garments that were tattered from too many washings.

What would you have done?

Let me put it this way: these examples quickly con-vinced me that, if death came suddenly and without warning, who could manage to follow the intention of "a dying tiger leaves its skin intact"?

And that's why I envy chronically ill patients and old folks nearing the end of their lives, like Buñuel, for they have adequate time to make their preparations, since death is anticipated. I don't mean just writing a will or making their own funeral arrangements, stuff like that. What I'm saying is: they have enough time to decide what to burn and destroy and what to leave behind—the diaries, correspondence, photographs, and curious objects from idiosyncratic collecting habits they've treasured and kept throughout their lives.

For example, I was once asked by the heartbroken wife of a teacher who had died unexpectedly to go through the effects in his office. Among the mountains of research material on the Zhou dynasty city-state, I found a note-book recording the dates of conjugal bliss with his wife over the thirty years of their marriage. The dates were accompanied by complicated notations that were clearly secret codes, perhaps to describe the degree of satisfac-tion he'd achieved. I couldn't decide whether to burn it to protect the old man or treat it as a rare treasure and turn it over to his wife.

Actually, in addition to destroying things, I should also fabricate or arrange things in such a way that people would think what I wanted them to think about me. A minor ruse might be to obtain some receipts for charitable donations or copy down some occasional, personal notes that are more or less readable and might even be self-published by the surviving family. Even more delicate was a case I once read about in the health and medical section of the newspaper: a gramps in his seventies who had a penile implant wrote to ask if he should have it removed before emigrating to mainland China, for he was afraid that, after he died and was cremated, his children and grandchildren would discover his secret from the curious object that neither burned nor melted.

So you need to understand that the advance preparations I'm talking about go far beyond passive procedures to prevent becoming a nameless vegetable or an anonymous corpse; in fact, they have developed into an exquisite, highly proactive state.

I decided to begin by attending to my wallet.

The first thing I threw away was the sloppy-looking dental floss; then I tossed some business cards I'd taken out of politeness from people whose names I could no longer remember, a few baffling but colorful paper clips, a soft drink pull-tab to exchange for a free can, a book coupon, etc. In sum, a bunch of junk whose only significance was to show how shabby I was.

What then are the things that are both meaningful and fully explanatory, and are reasonably found in a wallet?

First of all, my career does not require business cards, and I had no employee ID card or work permit. I didn't have a driver's license and hadn't joined any serious organization or recreational club, so I had no membership cards. I didn't even have a credit card!

—Speaking of credit cards, they create a mystery that causes considerable consternation. I'm sure you've experienced this: you're in a department store or a large shop or a restaurant, and the cashier asks, "Cash or charge?"

Based on my observations, even though the cashier's tone is usually neutral and quite proper, those who pay cash stammer their response, while those who pay with a credit card answer loud and clear. Isn't that weird? Aren't the credit card users, simply put, debtors? The implication, at least, is: I have the money to pay you, but for now, or for the next few weeks, the credit guarantee system of my bank lets me owe you without having to settle up.

But what about those who pay cash? They are able to hand over the money with one hand and take possession of the goods with the other, with neither party owing the other a thing. Why then should they be so diffident? And what makes those paying with a credit card so self-assured?

Could it be that the latter, after a credit check to prove that they are now and in the future will continue to be productive, can enter the system and be completely trusted? And the former, those who owe nothing to anyone, why are they so irretrievably timid? Is it possible they cannot be incorporated into the control system of an industrial, commercial society because their mode of production or their productivity is regarded as somehow uncivilized, unscientific, and unpredictable, the equivalent of an agricultural-age barter system? Simply put, when you are not a cog with a clearly defined purpose and prerequisite in the system, their trust in you is based on what they can see, and that must be a one-time exchange of money and goods, since there is no guarantee of exchange credit for the next time, or the time after that. You are neither trusted nor accepted by a gigantic, intimidating system, and that is why you are diffident, timid, even though you could well be able and diligent, and are not necessarily poor, at least not a beggar or a homeless person who pays no taxes.

By contrast, those whose wallets are choked with cards of every kind are trusted by organizations, big and small, which vie to admit them and consider them indispensable. They are so complacent, so confident, and all because: "I have credit, therefore I am."

Can a person living in this world be without a name, or a dwelling place?

My wallet was empty, with nothing to fill it up and no way to disguise that, but I didn't want the person who opened it to see at first glance that it belonged to one of life's losers. So I put in a few thousand-NT bills, which I wouldn't use for so long they'd begin to look as if they were part of the wallet itself.

The wallet may have been empty, but since it wouldn't hold a passport, I debated whether to include my ID card to establish my identity—when 20 million ID cards are attached to 20 million people, you see, the meaning is nullified—and I could not follow your suggestion to, in a feigned casual manner, insert a small note with my name and phone number on it. Which meant that putting aside the issue of becoming a nameless vegetable or an anonymous corpse on the sidewalk, this anonymous wallet would, sooner or later, become nonreturnable, even if found by a Samaritan.

Ah! A savorless, flavorless, colorless, odorless wallet. Sometimes I pretended to be a stranger, examining and fondling it, speculating how the Samaritan who found it would sigh emotionally: "What an uninteresting and unimportant person your owner must be!"

After I lost interest in the disguise and the construction of my wallet, for a while I turned my attention to my clothes. Especially my underwear. To be ready for an unexpected sexual encounter—no, I mean for the unannounced visit of death.

Underwear is very important, and it's not enough just to keep it from becoming tattered or turning yellow. On psychological, social, even political levels, it describes its owner more vividly than many other things. Didn't Bill Clinton respond shyly that his underpants weren't those trendy plaid boxers, but were skin-hugging briefs?

And just look at his foreign policy!

Still, I gave serious consideration to changing and washing my underwear religiously, and to the purchase of new sets. For starters, I tossed my black and purple sets, along with my Clinton-style briefs, all of which might have caused undue speculation. After mulling over the replacements, I decided to go to the open-rack garment section of Watson's, where no salesperson would bother me, and picked out several pairs of white Calvin Klein 100 percent cotton underpants, though their yuppie style didn't quite match my antisocial tendencies. My significant other was all but convinced I had a new love interest, and we had a big fight over that. But I didn't reveal the truth. If one day

I happened to depart this world before him, then my clear, white underwear would remind that grief-stricken man of what I looked like after my shower on so many nights. Those sweet memories might comfort him, at least a little.

But my preparatory work didn't end there.

On some days, when I had to go to work, I passed the site where I'd nearly fallen, knowing full well that the strength that had sustained me and would not let me fall came from the thought: "I'll not be randomly discovered and identified like this."

Randomly discovered. In addition to the state I was in, the wallet, my clothes, there was also location. That's right, location. I thought back carefully to the routes I took when I went out and realized that, even though I was in the habit of roaming a bit, there was a definite sense of order and, in the end, it would be easy for a secret agent, even a neophyte P.I., to follow me. Even so, I strove to simplify my routes, avoiding places that would be hard to explain, even if I was just passing by.

Let me put it this way. An upright, simple, extremely religious, and highly disciplined college classmate of mine died in a fire at a well-known sex sauna last year. The fire-fighters found him, neatly dressed, dead of asphyxiation, in the hallway. We went to give our condolences to his wife, also a college classmate, and as we warmly recalled all the good deeds he'd performed when alive and said he'd definitely be ushered into heaven, we couldn't completely shake the subtle sense of embarrassment—what exactly was the good fellow, our classmate, doing there?

We could not ask, and she could not answer.

So I was determined to avoid vulgar, tasteless little

local temples, shrouded in incense smoke; I didn't want to die in front of a spirit altar, giving my significant other the impression I'd changed religions.

And I didn't want to go to the Ximen-ding area, which I'd pretty much avoided since graduating from college, afraid I'd end up dead in an area honeycombed with dilapidated sex-trade alleys, fall under suspicion, like that good classmate of mine, and be unable to defend myself.

From then on, I quickened my steps whenever I walked by some of my favorite deep-green alleys, with their Japanese-style houses, where time seemed to stand still. I no longer stopped or strolled there, afraid that my significant other would suspect I'd hidden away an illegitimate child or was having a secret rendezvous with an old flame.

I even stopped roaming wherever my feet took me, as I'd done when I was younger, just so I wouldn't be found dead on a beach where people came to watch the sunset. Otherwise, my credit card-carrying significant other would be embroiled in a lifelong puzzle and be mired in deep grief.

After all, death only visits us once in our lifetime, so we should make advance preparations for its arrival.

> *Hundreds of years ago, the Man of La Mancha*
> *howled at the sky—*
> *A windblown quest*
> *Seeking love in steel and rocks*
> *Using manners with savages*

And me, afraid that the handwriting would be eaten away by mites and no longer legible, I wrote this down.

Translated by Howard Goldblatt

The Floating City
Xi Xi

I. THE FLOATING CITY

The floating city appeared suddenly before everyone's eyes in the middle of the sky like a hydrogen-filled balloon on a clear, bright day many years ago. Rolling clouds swirled by above; waves crashed on the swelling sea below. The floating city hovered, going neither up nor down as it maintained its position, buffeted slightly by the breeze.

Only our grandparents' grandparents witnessed how it all began. It had been an unbelievable and terrifying experience, one they recalled fearfully. There had been a violent collision of clouds lighting up the sky with flashes and roars of thunder. On the sea countless pirate vessels

XI XI (1938–) was born on the mainland, but has spent most of her life in Hong Kong, which has often been the focus of her many works of fiction. She began her career as a writer in the 1970s, but became well known only in the 1980s. Her novel *My City* (1979) is representative of her fiction about Hong Kong, as is the short story presented here. "The Floating City" (1988) presents sketches of Hong Kong that wonderfully capture the city's distinct cultural hybridity and its traumatic struggle to define its identity in the transition from British colony to its "return" to the motherland.

had run up the skull and crossbones and fired their cannon nonstop. Suddenly the floating city had dropped from the clouds and hung in midair.

Many years passed. Our grandparents' grandparents passed away, and our grandparents followed them into a deep sleep. By and by the story they had told became a mysterious legend.

The grandchildren settled in the city and gradually adapted to living there. Even its legend faded. Finally, the majority of people came to believe that the floating city had always hung in the sky, neither rising nor sinking. Even when it was buffeted by the wind and shook ever so slightly, it was like swinging on a swing.

Many more years passed.

2. THE MIRACLE

It takes courage to live without roots: That's what it said on the jacket of a novel. To live in the floating city required not only courage, but willpower and faith. In another novel there is a nonexistent knight who is nothing more than an empty suit of armor. Emperor Charlemagne asks him, what keeps you going? Willpower and faith, he replies.

With their willpower and faith, the inhabitants of the floating city toiled to create a livable home. Within a few dozen years their efforts made the city vibrant, prosperous, and wealthy. Buildings stood packed together in rows on the ground; highways and overpasses writhed in the air. Trains like centipedes ran underground and out to the suburbs; kidney stones were destroyed with laser beams; tumors could be located with brain scanners; people could follow the course of Halley's Comet in the observatory;

and the life of the sea lion was an open book in the ocean park. Children were provided with nine years of free education, and there were unemployment benefits for the jobless, pensions for the disabled and elderly. Many arts festivals were held each year, and books from all over the world were available in the stores. If you didn't want to talk to anyone, there was absolute freedom to be silent.

People couldn't quite believe it possible that houses in the city could float in midair, that one flower grown there could fill a whole room. They all said that the floating city was a miracle.

3. SHOWERS

May to September was the windy season. The winds blew from all directions, and the floating city swayed in the sky. The residents of the floating city were used to the swaying, and they went about their business as usual, not even missing the races. They knew from experience that the floating city would never be blown upsidedown or in circles during the windy season, nor would it be blown away to some other place.

But one peculiar thing did happen in the windy season: The people dreamed. They started dreaming in May; they dreamed the same dream; they dreamed they were floating in the air, neither rising nor falling. It was as though each of them was a floating city in miniature. None of them had wings, so they couldn't fly, they could only float. They didn't speak to one another. They floated in absolute, solemn silence. Every day the sky in the floating city was full of floating people, just like rain in April.

From May on, people dreamed about floating. Even people who slept during the day dreamed that they had turned into floating people standing silently in midair. These dreams went away only in September. After the windy season people started having their own dreams once more.

Why did everyone have the same dream? Why did they all dream they were floating in the sky? One school of psychologists came to the conclusion that this was the collective expression of a "Third Riverbank Neurosis."

4. APPLES

In the summer a poster appeared in the streets of the floating city. On it was a picture of an apple with a line of French above it. It said: *"Ceci n'est pas une pomme"* — "This is not an apple." The appearance of the poster was not unusual since a large art exhibition was going to be held. This year's exhibition was being held in honor of the Belgian artist Rene Magritte. The apple was one of his paintings.

What did "This is not an apple" mean? The picture was obviously of an apple. What the artist had meant was that the painting of an apple was not the same as an apple you can eat. You couldn't touch it, smell it, or cut its flesh. It wasn't a real apple; it was made up of lines, color, and forms. The apple in the painting was an illusion. Didn't the Greek philosopher Plato say that even the best, most realistic painting of a bed is still only a reproduction of a bed?

Posters of Magritte's painting could be seen on every street corner, although only one or two out of every thousand people in the floating city would actually go to see the exhibition. The appearance of so many apples in the streets of the floating city was nonetheless a cause for excitement. Many people mistook it for an advertisement for the fruit market. Only a few intellectuals suddenly thought to themselves: The floating city is a stable place that neither rises nor sinks, yet it, too, is an illusion. The miracle of the floating city was not, after all, a fairy tale.

5. THE EYE

"Cinderella" is a fairy tale. The pumpkin turns into a carriage; mice turn into horses; Cinderella's rags turn into a ball gown. But at midnight everything turns back into what it was. Was the floating city just another Cinderella?

The people of the floating city didn't have defective eyes. Modern science provided them with the most accurate microscopes and telescopes. They often looked down at the sea or upward at the sky and tested the direction of the wind. Why could the floating city continue to float steadily in the sky? Was it due to the gravitational pull between the sea and the sky? Or was Fate holding countless invisible strings and putting on a puppet show?

The apple in the picture was not a real apple; the city that existed so miraculously might not remain stable forever. But could the floating city control its own destiny? The instant the pull between the sea and the sky changed, or Fate tired of its game, wouldn't the city sink, rise, or perhaps be blown off to some unknown place?

The people of the floating city opened their eyes wide and looked down. The angry waves of the sea surged beneath their feet. The city could be overwhelmed by the waters. Even if it managed to float on the water, wouldn't there be a massacre when the pirates flying the skull and crossbones fell on them in droves? If the floating city rose upward, would the shifting, airy clouds provide a stable foundation for its solid weight?

6. A PROBLEM

The floating city did not have any rivers, and the sea water was undrinkable. The city had to rely on the bounty of heaven for water. So although the people of the floating city liked brilliant sunny days, sometimes they had to pray for rain.

A teacher took a class of students to the exhibition hall of the Town Hall. They'd come for the art show. The students had pens and paper so they could record their impressions and copy down the names of the paintings. They asked: What does the picture of an umbrella with a glass full of water on it mean? And why is it called *Hegel's Holiday*? They looked through the exhibition catalogue hoping to find an answer.

People treat water in different ways at different times. Sometimes they are tolerant of it, sometimes they reject it. For example, people want to drink water when they are thirsty, they want it inside them. But on rainy days they use umbrellas to keep it out. Internal and external acceptance and rejection are things philosophers often think about. As for the problem of water, perhaps the philosopher Hegel might have been interested in giving it some thought. But it was a small problem, one he reserved for his holidays.

One student stood looking at this painting for a long time. He said: People use umbrellas to keep themselves dry. Since the water is all in the glass, there's no need for an umbrella. There's no need to reject anything. If there were a solid, reliable layer of clouds over the floating city, there would be hope for the city if it floated upward. Why reject it?

7. THE FLOWER SPIRIT

The majority of the residents of the floating city were men who wore hats—the symbol of the petit bourgeoisie. They desired a stable, prosperous society, a warm, happy home. So they worked industriously every day; they were as busy as ants or bees. Hard work can help you forget lots of things. As a result of their labors, the people of the floating city were able to build a wealthy modern society in which everyone was well fed and well dressed. But it was a society in which material attractions were so great that people threw themselves into their labors with ever greater energy. They became victims of the bottomless pit of material desire.

One painting by the Italian Renaissance artist Botticelli is called *Primavera;* it shows a goddess scattering flowers over the earth and symbolizes the return of spring. The messenger Hermes leads the way; Cupid flies above Venus; the West Wind accompanies the Flower Spirit; and the Three Graces dance around as Primavera, dressed in fine colored gauzes, scatters fragrant blossoms.

Li Gonglin of the Song dynasty painted a work entitled *Vimalakirti Preaching* that shows Manjusri with some disciples visiting the sick Vimalakirti at the Buddha's command. Despite his illness, Vimalakirti is preaching the dharma and enunciating the essence of the Great Vehicle to them. While he speaks, a heavenly spirit releases a shower of flowers. Manjusri's chief disciple is covered with the blossoms.

The citizens of the rich and populous floating city were so enamored of material wealth that they wished the heavenly spirit would cast all of her flowers onto them; they even wished they could bundle Primavera up with her flowers in a sack and carry it around with them.

8. TIME

It was an important moment, an absolute point in time. A train engine had just pulled in. A moment earlier the engine had not yet entered the fireplace; a moment later, it would have gone. It was only when the engine was steaming through the fireplace, only at this absolute point in time, that the smoke from its stack could go up the chimney. The chimney was the only suitable conduit for the smoke.

The fireplace reminded one of Christmas, a day the whole city celebrated. However, judging from the room this was not Christmas, because there were no stockings hanging in front of the fireplace, no pine tree in the room, no bright lights, no angels, no bells, no candles in bronze candle holders.

On the marble clock on the mantelpiece the hour hand was approaching one, the minute hand was approaching nine. It was unclear where the second hand was. It was after midnight. A carriage would be a pumpkin again by now, horses would have turned back into mice, and the ball gown would be rags once more.

Yes, it was after midnight. But all the fables said that Cinderella would meet her prince on a white horse before midnight. Had the prince of the floating city been waiting close by as midnight approached? Although he was riding a magic white horse, since it had only one horsepower, perhaps he had arrived late.

Zero hour always made people anxious. What would it be like at one o'clock? Could people see the future through the mirror?

9. THE MIRROR

Only people who have been to the floating city will appreciate that the mirrors there are different. In "Snow White and the Seven Dwarfs" a magic mirror hangs in the wicked queen's palace. It can answer questions and tell the queen who is the fairest of them all. It is an honest, sincere mirror: It never lies. The mirrors in the floating city are also honest mirrors. They reflect reality without fear or favor. Yet they have their limitations: The mirrors in the floating city can reflect only the backs of things.

All the mirrors, whether produced locally or imported, reflect only the reverse side of things. Whenever the people in the floating city look in a mirror, all they can see is the hair on the back of their heads. People have experimented by putting another mirror in front of the mirror on the wall, but no matter what they do, no matter how many mirrors are used and at whatever angles, they show only the backs of things. Women in the floating city always have to go to the beauty parlor to get made up because it is too difficult to do it themselves. If the men want a good shave, they have to go to a barber.

In the floating city's mirrors you can't find any answers or forecast the future. But you can know the past, and this isn't necessarily a bad thing. History can teach lessons, and this is one of the good things about the mirrors in the floating city.

10. WINGS

There are many means of transportation in the floating city: some ancient, like rope ladders and balloons, some modern, such as helicopters and parachutes. People who want to have a look in the clouds can climb the ladders or go up by balloon, while visitors to the sea can use parachutes or go by helicopter. However, over half of the people in the floating city want to grow wings themselves. All in all, these people find it scary to live in a city that floats in midair. The people who are really terrified agonize night and day, finally deciding to pack up their belongings and they behave like migratory birds, moving elsewhere to build an ideal new nest.

A novelist has recorded the following story: A man went to apply for a passport. The official asked where he wanted to go. He said it didn't matter. The official gave him a globe of the world and asked him to make his choice. The man studied it, turned it around slowly, and finally said: Don't you have another one?

It is a difficult decision to know where to go once you've left the floating city. Where can you find a city where you could live in peace forever? All those leaving the city have to have very strong wings, and they have to be very careful when in flight. If they go too near the sun, the wax that keeps the wings together melts and, like Icarus, they plummet to earth.

But the residents of the floating city are not really like migratory birds. Once they leave they do not return. Can they just go away, holding a walking stick and carrying their luggage, without ever looking back? Although the people in the floating city long to be like the pigeons that fly high in the sky, they are frustrated like birds imprisoned in a cage.

11. BIRD GRASS

In their longing to fly, the people of the floating city keep looking up at the sky. But they can't take off, nor can they create a hoist to lift them into the sky. All they can do is dream when the windy season approaches, dream that they can float silently in the air. Even in their dreams they float but cannot fly.

After the windy season all of them dream their own dreams once more. They dream of bean-curd kites, snowflakes filling the sky, butterflies, thistledown in the wind. Some people even dream that the city itself has grown wings. But they always wake up to find their feet still firmly on the ground of the floating city. And from that ground is born one of the strangest plants in the whole world, something never seen anywhere before: bird grass.

Bird grass, with its dark, lush foliage, grows everywhere—in the city and outside, on the banks of brooks, in valleys and gardens. It is a peculiar plant with large, flat, bird-shaped leaves. If you pick a leaf, it is easy to make out a bird's head, beak, and eyes. The fuzz on the leaf is like feathers. The leaves rustle in the soft breeze, like the beating of wings.

Although shaped like birds, it is still only grass. None of the bird grass has wings. People say if it grew wings it would be able to fly. The air of the floating city would be full of flying bird grass, and no one would be able to tell whether it was birds or grass, animal or vegetable.

12. THE CHILD PRODIGIES

The child prodigies appeared in the same year as the bird grass. At first they attracted no special attention; they were simply milk-guzzling babies. But they grew quickly, both physically and mentally. Before long they were healthy, precocious children.

Possibly it began with arithmetic. The mothers noticed that none of them used pen or paper to do their sums, they used colored blocks of wood. They knew to use meters to measure cloth and grams to buy rice. And what was set theory? Gradually the mothers found they couldn't understand their children's textbooks. The children didn't have to open their books to study, they just turned on the television or put earphones on their ears.

At first the children told their mothers to keep the window open when using the gas water heater to have a bath and not to use too much salt when cooking; later they took their mothers on trips, treated them to meals, and gave them presents. The mothers felt as though they were becoming the children. The children ruled the family, taking over the mother's position as the head of the family, overthrowing their traditional authority. Many mothers felt scared and didn't know what to do.

A few mothers were happy with the situation. They had been plagued by doubts and worries and had faced many unresolved problems. Now their brilliant children would, perhaps, solve all these problems for them.

13. WINDOWS

The earth is only one small planet in the universe. The floating city is only one small city on the earth. On a map it is no larger than the head of a pin, and it did not even seem to have a name. But gradually this tiny city attracted attention from afar.

The strange city floating in the air with its mirrors that

reflected only the backs of things, its people who dreamed of floating in the windy season, the bird grass that grew in its soil attracted endless numbers of tourists. They came to explore, to experience, to see their reflections in the mirrors, and to dream. People who didn't come were also curious; they stood outside the city and looked in through the windows, their arms hanging by their sides. Obviously they could afford no practical assistance, but their gazing was a form of participation. Looking on was a kind of supervision.

What did the observers outside the windows see now? They saw a teacher with a group of students at Town Hall for the Magritte exhibition. Small groups of people were gathered in front of the paintings hanging on the walls. Suddenly the observers outside and the students and teachers who were looking at the paintings inside saw one another. You could follow the subtle development of events from the solemn expressions on the faces of the observers. If it was a tragedy, their faces would show sorrow; if a comedy, they would light up with a smile.

Over there, employees were putting up posters of the Mona Lisa on the announcement boards. Over here, the people in the painting and the people looking at the painting were staring at one another through an open window, all thinking their own thoughts.

Translated by Geremie R. Barmé and Linda Jaivin

Fish!

Alai

OWING TO A MINOR ILLNESS, I stayed in the town of Tanggor to rest and do some writing for three days. A few doses of anti-inflammatory medicine put me back on my feet, and my three companions circled round to pick me up. Once we were back on the road, our Jeep headed west alongside the Yellow River. The morning sun glinted off of our reflectors. The rumble of the engine and the vibrations of the tires on the smooth highway traveled up to my hands through the steering wheel, and I felt my

ALAI (1959–) is of mixed ethnic heritage—Tibetan and Hui Muslim. He grew up in the culturally mixed area of Aba, in northwestern Sichuan, a region whose unique culture has been shaped by Tibet to its west and the Han Chinese to the east. His best-known novel, translated into English as *Red Poppies* (original novel published in 1998), won the Mao Dun prize for literature in 2000. It focuses on the impact of modernity in this borderland region between Tibet and Sichuan. "Fish!" (2000) presents an almost surrealist account of a trip into the Songpan marsh in the area's high mountain plateau, where the first-person narrator—a Tibetan—fishes for carp, despite the Tibetan taboo against it. The story seems to raise complex issues about ethnic identity, a recurrent theme in Alai's fiction.

strength returning. After we'd driven some forty or fifty kilometers, the road veered off the broad grassy riverbank and began to climb.

I stopped halfway up a hill to turn the wheel over to our assigned driver.

Everyone climbed out of the Jeep, stretched, and squinted as we all aimlessly took in our surroundings. The town we'd just left had nearly disappeared in the deepest part of the prairie, the distance giving it an aura of beauty it didn't really possess. The bright sunshine lent slight warmth to the broad, gently flowing river at the foot of the hill. We sat on the ground, a soft rustle emerging from the autumn grass around us. That was the sound of the last thin layer of frost evaporating. The air was saturated with the fragrance of drying grass. After a cigarette break, we stood up, brushed the crushed grass off the seats of our pants, and were about to set out, when the rotund rump of a sleek-skinned animal lumbered into view. It was a giant marmot heading back to its dry mountain den after drinking from the river. The thick autumn grass parted as it made its way up the hill, and then closed behind it. I fetched my small-bore rifle from the car, took aim at the swaying movements of the inviting rump, and fired. The explosion flew off into the distance on the sun's rays, the fresh, stirring smell of gunpowder fining our nostrils. The marmot vanished without a trace, and I thought I'd hit it. But there was no blood at the spot where it had leaped at the sound before disappearing.

We climbed back into the Jeep and headed down the hill, continuing along the broad, grassy banks of the Yellow River until noon, when we started up another incline, where we stopped for lunch. On a big piece of army canvas, we laid out bottles of beer, some beef jerky, and some hardtack we'd bought at a Muslim café in a prairie town. Then, after eating our fill, we indulged in the languid pleasure of simply lying in the dry autumn grass. Warm, clean rays of sunlight from high in the boundless blue sky washed down on our hair, eyes, and bodies, like a special kind of bath. As windblown grass gently caressed our faces and hands, we felt as soft and spongy, body and soul, as the rich prairie soil beneath us. Crisscrossing streams at the foot of the hill fed placid bogs here and there, their watery surfaces glinting in the sunlight. They looked every bit as warm and as yielding as our sun-drenched bodies.

Inexplicably, I had a vision of the fish swimming lazily in all that water.

The ridges of their backs were black, their bellies light yellow. They made no sound as they hung suspended tranquilly beneath the surface, like dreamy shadows. Lacking scales on their bodies, they were known as naked carp. In the early nineteenth century, the Zoige and other local prairies were known collectively as the Songpan Prairie, and the fish were called Songpan naked carp. While I lay there lost in thought, my companions took fishing line, hooks, and bait out of the trunk of the Jeep Cherokee. As with rifles and ammunition, these are essential items for travel on the prairie.

We four had been sent out as a religious survey team, but were taking a break to get in some hunting and fishing. Two of my companions decided to head up the hill to hunt wild rabbits and marmots, leaving Gongpo Tashi and me to fish in the river.

Fishing was definitely the wrong assignment for me.

Water burials are common out on the prairie. Water and the fish that swim in it relieve the soul of its mortal body, which is why many Tibetans consider fish taboo. For this trip, I'd taken along a book sent to me by Professor Dhondup Wangbum of the Central Institute of Nationalities. Included in this book on popular Tibetan taboos and nature worship was a discussion of the taboo against catching and eating fish. The author wrote that in traditional rituals for exorcising ghosts and other unclean entities, it is essential to direct the incantations at invisible malevolent objects, driving them off of dry land, out of places of abode, and away from the depths of the heart straight into water. As a result, fish are a repository for inauspicious entities. Of course, I'd witnessed such rituals of exorcism and incantation, but had never linked them to the taboo against fish. And while the Tibetan tradition of neither catching nor eating fish has a long history, in the second half of the twentieth century, we began eating fish, and I confess that I am one of those fish-eating Tibetans. Still, what others describe as the mouthwatering tenderness of fish seems somehow rancid in my mouth.

And so, today's division of labor could not have been less appropriate.

The two Han Chinese, for whom the taboo against fish did not exist, picked up their rifles and began climbing at a crouch, the hilly expanse opening up ahead of them, while I followed Tashi down to the riverbank. The grassy ground at our feet rose and fell unevenly, since the prairie actually served as a covering for marshy earth below. Although the sky was so clear I could see for miles around, the bumpy ground and the menacing gurgles from the mud below unnerved this first-time fisherman.

Ever fished before? Tashi asked.

I shook my head. I was about to ask him the same thing. There was a hard edge to his obvious disappointment as he said, Well, I thought you had!

I didn't ask why he'd thought that, of course, since in the eyes of so many of my sinicized countrymen, I'm a bit more sinicized than they are, simply because I write in Chinese. Now that we were about to become fishermen, he must have assumed that I was more experienced than he.

Honest? Tashi asked again. You've never fished?

I shook my head vigorously.

He thrust the can of bait into my hand. Then I'm going hunting with the others. His powerful frame nearly flew across the grassy bank, nimbly yet with obvious reserves of strength, crossing one marshy spot and one little stream after another. The way he ran could make you swear he could race a cheetah if he had to. But now he'd placed all that power in the service of escape.

I stopped alongside a stream.

This particular stream was so shallow that the sun's rays dappled the riverbed. The banks were covered with red and white saw grass floating on the surface of the water. Shifting sand on the bottom, and not the water itself, produced a constant murmur. It was not a wide stream; in fact, it was squeezed so tightly at this spot that I could easily jump across it. I broke off a willow branch, tied on a line and some hooks, and was ready to fish.

What nearly stopped me was baiting the hooks. I opened the jar, and there, squirming in the rich black dirt and green leaves, were fat worms as thick as my pinkie. When I picked one up and pinched it in two, sticky muck oozed out, a mixture of red and green, and stuck to my fingers. Since the line came with two hooks, after baiting the first, I had to do it again—once I'd wiped my hands clean on the grass, that is. I heaved a sigh of relief after the second hook was baited; by then, my forehead was beaded with sweat.

I cast my line in what I thought was practiced style. Unfortunately, the stream was so narrow that the hooks and the worms impaled on them, plus a small lead weight, carried the line whistling over to the opposite bank, where it landed in the grass. Then, in jerking the pole back, I lost one of my worms, which, meant I had to kill yet another one. With rising disgust, I watched as its sticky juices soiled my fingers again. The stuff was dark green, with some bright red spots. The color was less offensive after I put on my sunglasses. This time the hook landed in the water, and I watched as the bait slithered through one dappled beam of sunlight after another before coming to rest on the clear bottom. Then it followed the sand drifting downstream. Tossing my army knapsack, with its bait, hooks, and what have you, over my shoulder, I followed the progress of the worms.

In the flow of the water, the worms quickly disintegrated; the gooey insides were the first to go, leaving behind shreds of pale skin, until they too floated off. That brought an end to the material essence of worm. Every couple of hundred meters, as I made my way downstream, I had to stop to rebait my hooks. By the fifth or sixth time, I managed to calmly and casually pinch the worms and impale them on the hooks, causing hardly any distress, from my hands all the way up to my heart.

Two crisp gunshots from the far-off hill rocketed past me, hugging the ground as if they were the actual bullets. Even at that distance, I could see my companions running up the hill in the wake of the echoing gunshots. My hooks settled heavily in the water, the thin sound of shifting pebbles whispering in my ears. The last drops of moisture on the autumn grass hissed softly as they turned to mist. The water tugged gently at my line, the light quivers of the pole traveling down to my hand. The willow branch was rough on the skin, so I switched it to my other hand, and immediately felt the lingering heat from the sun. My companions had split up and were now making their way through the underbrush. Obviously, their shots had missed their target, allowing the marmot to return safely to its home. A moment later, green smoke curled skyward, the three men slipping in and out of the haze. They must have been choking as they stood around the opening trying to fan smoke down into the marmot's lair, hoping that would drive it out of its underground maze. But marmots build complex underground palaces, and even if this particular one had somehow neglected to equip its palace with ventilation tunnels, fanning smoke into a series of underground tunnels is a time-consuming process. Professional hunters always take air-blowers along with them. But not my companions, who were surely suffering more from their own smoke than the marmot ever would. At least where hunting land animals is concerned, I had plenty of experience.

Fishing was another matter altogether.

Suddenly I felt a tug. My heart skipped a heat. A fish? I looked down at the water. No longer lying on the bottom, the hooks and weight had been carried by the current to a spot not far from where I was standing, where the water formed a sizeable whirlpool. A noise like that of an ox being slaughtered rose from the whirlpool, the death rattle emerging from deep in its throat. It was a sound I sometimes heard from one of the city sewers. My hook had been sucked into the whirlpool, and when I tugged on the line, it tugged back.

Fish!

Enlightened lamas of the True Word sect once told me that when they are alone in their meditation chambers they have visions of a gleaming Tibetan word or some other image. I'd never been a True Word devotee, but the word *fish* streaked through my head, minus the gleam.

Fish! The word was swathed in the sticky sleek grayness of a scaleless body that, for some strange reason, instilled terror in me.

I heard myself blurt out the word, less from happiness than from amazement: Fish!

Just then a hulking fish broke the surface and whipped its glistening, watery body in the air; at the moment it left the life-sustaining water, it seemed caught up in feverish joy. Once I loosened my grip, the fish landed in the grass, and the watery sheen on its body vanished, replaced by a sticky sleek grayness. It was a color pregnant with misgivings. The closer I got to the fish, the stronger my sense of decay.

This was the first fish I'd ever caught.

Now that it was out of the water, it lay in the grass

without moving. I knew that removing the hook would be a grisly process, and didn't dare look into the fish's sad bulging eyes. I gazed up into the sky instead, and as scattered puffy clouds floated in my eyes, I picked it up. It slipped right out of my hand. I don't know if that was because the fish put up a fight, or because its illusory slipperiness made me open my hand. It lay on its side in the grass, its mouth opening and closing frantically. Bloody froth gathered at the corners. The look of sadness in eyes that still somehow showed that it was resigned to its fate grew faint. Dropping the fish, of course, meant that I had to pick it up out of the grass again; this time I squeezed it so hard, its sharp fin cut my palm, and as I removed the hook from deep in its throat, its watery blood mixed with the thick blood from my cut hand.

Having watched other people fish out on the prairie, I knew that I ought now to snap off a flexible willow twig and thread it through one of the gills and out the mouth. That way I could string together all my fish, making it easy to carry the day's catch home. But all I'd really wanted to do was catch *a* fish on the prairie, not a whole string of them. That was why I'd been drawn to this shallow stream. Not far off, a river worthy of the name raised whitecaps as it rushed along.

Now the problem was, I'd caught a fish in my shallow stream without even trying! That was the last thing in the world I'd desired.

After rebaiting the hooks, I walked back and gazed at the spot where the fish had emerged. I saw nothing out of the ordinary. A little eddy, that's all, with the death rattle of the slaughtered ox vanishing into the grass at my feet.

I stomped down hard, and the grass rustled briefly before returning to its stony silence. With surprising accuracy, I cast my hooks directly into the whirlpool. The bait made a few turns on the surface before sinking to the bottom.

It had no sooner disappeared from sight than my hand felt as if it had been stung, and the pole nearly flew out of my hand. Instinctively, I jerked it back, raising a raucous little geyser in the water. Another fish soared heavily through the air, and as it passed over my head in the sun's glare, its belly turned from the jaundiced yellow of earth to a blinding golden color. The shout that escaped from my lips could have been one of fright and could have been one of joy. This time the fish was separated from the hook in its mouth as it flew through the air and landed in the grass. It was lying there without moving by the time I reached it. The glare in its bulging eyes sent chills down my spine.

I returned to my spot alongside the stream and cast my hook. A fish took the bait almost immediately.

In hardly any time at all, I pulled a dozen fish out from under that whirlpool, one right after the other. They looked like a group of young adults, all the same age. I gazed down at them strewn across the grassy ground, and then turned to look at the marshy bogs around me, silent except for an occasional air bubble breaking the surface. I had the uneasy feeling that I was conspiring in the death wish of hordes of fish that had gathered in the same unlikely spot. A conspiracy! But this thought zoomed out of my head through a force of will. If I'd let it settle in, I might never have another chance to break free from the cultural taboo against fish.

We act so as not to have to stop and think about what we're doing.

My activity on this day was to cast baited hooks into a little pool (I'm convinced that a small but deep pool lay hidden beneath the stream's grassy covering), wanting to see how many stupid fish were waiting to fling themselves into the jaws of death. In the autumn fish settle low in the water, fat and lazy, and greedily swallow baited hooks all the way down to their stomachs. I turned to look at the fish lying lazily in the grass, waiting to die, and a strange mixture of loathing and fear surged inside me.

Inexplicably, I added another hook to the line and baited all three. They drifted slowly out to the center and were sucked down into the pool that may or may not have existed. I took a few deep breaths to calm myself. At the same time, I tried to imagine the bait slowly settling in the seemingly bottomless stream, floating in front of a fish suspended motionless in the water. Somewhat disappointed, the bait continued its way down into the darker water. With thoughts of that descent, I felt myself get lighter, as if I were floating; the surrounding darkness frightened me. But just as I was about to take my line Out of the water, a fish pounced on the bait. Why, I wondered, had it attacked the bait so ferociously? Even if it was seeking death, there was no need to try so hard. It swallowed the bait and the hook hidden within it, then stopped moving and went still. I waited. A second fish took another hook, and then lay suspended calmly in the water, no fight in it, and no desire to escape death.

The third piece of bait went unswallowed.

Knowing I'd feel it if another fish bit, I turned to take a leisurely look at my companions on the distant hill, still pointlessly trying to smoke out the marmot. The smoke had thinned out, so apparently they'd abandoned their futile labor and had begun digging at the hole with an army-issue hoe we'd brought with us. If anything, this was even harder work, since the marmot's underground lair would begin a meter or so underground and then twist and snake along another hundred meters or two.

By all appearances a dull animal, the marmot is actually quite clever; by all appearances spry and responsive, these fish were unimaginably dull when confronted with a baited hook. See what I mean—a fish bit on the third hook! The pole bent nearly in half when I raised all three fish out of the water, and as they struggled, they all but pulled the pole into the stream. Their struggles were intended to return them to the water; that was something I could not agree to. With a shout and a mighty tug, I brought all three down onto the grass at my feet.

I took careful note as they stopped struggling the moment they hit the ground.

In fact, I took careful note of every facet of these fish, my prey. And not just careful note, but extremely careful note, with extreme sensitivity. I even took extremely careful and sensitive note of things that didn't exist.

At that moment, I took note of the cessation of struggle the moment the fish landed on the grassy ground. Some lay so close to the water that all they had to do was arch their backs, stiffen their bodies, and execute a flip any fish could manage to return to the stream. As the prairie turns a golden color, and the water begins to chill, flocks of migratory birds take wing. The fish, like a fleet of submarines, descend to the bottom of the stream, where there is little light but the water is warmer. As winter approaches, light is equated with freezing. But these fish, caught in the depths of the stream, now lay motionless in the grass, as if unaware that safety, that life itself, was so close. They lay there motionless, as if their deaths would test the limits of their killer's ability to justify his own actions. I was fishing that day in order to master myself. In this world we are often given incitements of many types, and mastering oneself is one of them. Mastering weaknesses in temperament, mastering a shyness or a fear of facing the unknown, mastering cultural or individual taboos. We then become unstoppable. I was now on my way to such mastery, and I wanted my companions to share in this moment. So I began waving my arms and shouting.

They stopped their laborious digging, straightened up, and stared in my direction. I picked up a fish and waved it in the air, shouting the whole time. They were a good two kilometers away, too far for them to see the fish in my hand, but I thought the sun glinting off its body would catch their attention. The sleek body did in fact glint in the sun's rays. The men were standing on the top of a little hill staring down at me, peaked rain clouds gathering in the sky at their backs. Lightning flashed from the clouds' dark, menacing centers, the sun adding a dazzling gold inlay to their edges. As thunder rumbled, the clouds moved eastward, toward us. Gusty breezes swept across the surface of the stream. The autumn grass, once standing proud, began to droop. And the wind caught my fishing line, which then formed a beautiful arc.

Another fish took a hook.

Deep down, I hoped it was the last one.

But then another one bit. Once again, I hoped it was

the last one, but I had no illusions, knowing there were plenty of fish down there in some secret spot prepared to come looking for death. I was right—a third fish was now on my line!

When the three fish left the water, they put up a brief, symbolic struggle before lying motionless on the grass with the others. With all those dying fish on the ground around me, even though the sun was shining, relatively mild gusts of wind sent chills through me.

I shouted at my companions again, wanting them to bring their stuff down the hill to gather up all my fish. I couldn't wait to leave the bank of this stream. How could there be so many big fish in such a little bit of water? It seemed to me as if they were taking the hooks faster and faster. I followed each new catch with a series of shouts to my companions.

The dark clouds overhead caught me by surprise. By this time, I was baiting my hooks and taking the fish out of the water like a machine, not because I was a greedy fisherman but because there were so many fish queuing up to die. I already knew there were lots of people in this world who had given up on life, but I hadn't realized that fish could also have a death wish. They wore the look of disciples of some evil cult, wanting to place the responsibility for taking their lives on others.

The loathing I felt was on the rise.

The roiling black clouds quickly formed an arch above me, turning the surface of the water dark and dreary. I must have worn a fiendish look as I flung my baited hooks into the little whirlpool. When the flowing water turned as dark and menacing as the rain clouds overhead, the spot began to look like the entrance to Hell. The fish continued to ardently take the path to death.

My companions made their way slowly down the hill, stepping carefully around the boggy spots. Not because of rumors that if you stepped in the wrong place, your foot would be sucked into the quicksand-like mud, and you would be pulled under, but because these citified country boys were afraid of soiling their nice shoes in the sticky, stinky mud.

My feelings of isolation and fear increased.

Thunder rumbled overhead. Winds that were growing stronger tore at my hair and my clothes; they also churned up the surface of the water. Large raindrops pelted me in the face. I opened my mouth to shout, but the wind drove the air right back down my throat. Meanwhile, the fish kept lining up, more than ever. How bizarre! This is incredible! The grinning god of death has shown his true colors! I heard myself say through clenched teeth, Come on, you fuckers!

I heard myself say tearfully, Come on, you fuckers, I'm not afraid of you!

I heard myself say, Don't tell me you're not afraid too! I'm afraid, but if you're not, then come on!

Just as I was about to go over the edge, it ended, not because there were no more fish in the pool, but because the tin bait box was empty. I slumped down on the ground, dejected, and let go of my fishing pole, which was carried off by the water. I might have been crying, I don't know, because the crackling thunder overhead covered all other sounds. Then it was the noise of an enormous rain cloud overhead crashing down on me. Then, no more thunder and no more lightning, at least not for the time being. The heaviness of dusk surrounded me. My companions and the prairie were wiped off the face of the earth. I couldn't even hear the wind. Oppressive darkness everywhere. And a terrifying calm. Autumn grass that only moments before had bent before the wind sprang up noisily. Then I heard a deep gurgle, sort of like the cooing of pigeons. But I knew at once it wasn't the sound of pigeons, it was . . . it was the fish!

The fish were shouting!

I'd never known that fish could do that!

But I was immediately aware that they were shouting! A strained, low sound: *Gurgle, gurgle.* Not the cries of pigeons, but a heart-stopping sound like that of stepping on a rotting piece of leather. When you step on leather like that, it's as if you're walking on a corpse. At that moment, all those half-dead fish were calling out. Staring with those damned eyes that never close and opening wide their thirsty mouths, they strained to gulp down the moist air saturated with the heavy odor of gunpowder. They gulped down a breath and then opened their mouths: *Gurgle.* Another breath and their mouths opened again: *Gurgle.*

All those ugly fish strewn across the grassy ground, first one opening its mouth—*gurgle*—then another—*gurgle.*

I didn't want to think what it would be like if it hadn't rained, so I sat there motionless. The cloud pushed the sky down low. I was afraid I might bump into it if I stood up, or be struck by a coil of lightning snaking through the roiling black cloud. Another crack of thunder made the ground beneath me lurch upward, followed by a torrent of rainwater mixed with sleet, as if dumped on my head from an enormous leather pouch. Stabs of pain restored my normal feelings.

When the sleet turned into a routine rainfall, I lay down on my belly and gratefully let it wash over me. It felt to me that I was having a good cry, something no one else would witness, and that even I might not completely understand. To this day, I don't know if my tears had mastered me or if I was crying because I had mastered myself. Or if I was crying over other things I should have cried over but hadn't.

Very quickly, a western wind began pushing back the black cloud, with its vast energy and abundant supply of water. The sun reappeared in the sky above all living creatures. Warmth slowly returned to my frozen body.

My three companions finally made it to where I was waiting.

They walked around picking up my catch and putting it into a willow basket, which, crammed full, required two men to carry it. When I pointed out for them the little whirlpool hidden beneath the floating grass, they refused to believe that all those fish could have come from that one spot. We changed out of our wet clothes in the Jeep; the smell of dry clothes, plus the car odors of plastic and gasoline, made me feel safe. Once we were back on the road, I turned to look at my fishing hole. With so many streams flowing across the prairie and glinting in the sunlight, I couldn't be sure which of them was the one where that improbable encounter had taken place. You see, before a person even takes leave of a spot where something has occurred, that event has already vanished into nothingness.

Translated by Howard Goldblatt

On the Oxcart
Xiao Hong

LATE MARCH. Clover covers the banks of the streams. In the early light of the morning our cart crushes the red and green grasses at the foot of the hill as it rumbles through the outskirts of Grandfather's village.

The carter is a distant uncle on Mother's side. He flicks his whip, but not to strike the rump of the ox; the tip merely dances back and forth in the air.

"Are you sleepy already? We've only just left the village!

XIAO HONG (1911–42) was born into a wealthy landlord family in the northeast province of Heilongjiang. Her father was abusive and family life was oppressive, so she left home at a young age, traveling first to nearby Harbin, then to Shanghai, where Lu Xun took her under his wing. Much of her fiction—especially *Tales of Hulan River* and *Field of Life and Death*—depict the suffering of women in the rural northeast. "On the Oxcart" was written in 1936, by which time the Japanese imperial army had come to occupy her native region. Ironically, Xiao was at the time living in Japan. The story expresses a kind of nostalgia for a lost homeland, yet there is a powerful tension between this nostalgia for the beautiful simplicity of place and the horror of Sister Wuyun's story of her husband's execution. Loss of family and loss of homeland are intertwined.

Drink some plum nectar now, and after we've crossed the stream ahead you can sleep." Grandfather's maid is on her way to town to visit her son.

"What stream? Didn't we just cross one?" The yellow cat we're bringing back from Grandfather's house has fallen asleep in my lap.

"The Houtang Stream."

"What Houtang Stream?" My mind is wandering. The only things from Grandfather's village still visible in the distance are the two gold balls on top of the red flagpole in front of the ancestral temple.

"Drink a cup of plum nectar, it'll perk you up," She is holding a cup of the dark yellow liquid in one hand as she puts the lid back on the bottle.

"I'm not going to need anything . . . perk me up? You perk yourself up!" They both laugh as the carter suddenly cracks his whip.

"You young lady, you . . . you sharp-tongued little scamp . . . I, I. . . ." He turns over from alongside the axle and reaches out to grab hold of my hair. Drawing my shoulders back, I clamber to the rear of the cart. Every kid in the village is scared of him. They say he used to be a soldier, and when he pinches your ear it hurts like the dickens. Sister Wuyun has gotten down off the cart to gather a lot of different kinds of flowers for me. Now the wind blowing in from the wildwood has picked up a bit, and her scarf is flapping around her head. I pretend that it's a raven or a magpie, like the ones I saw in the village. Look at 'er jumpin' up and down, just like a kid! She's back in the cart now, singing out the names of all kinds of flowers. I've never seen her so happy.

I can't tell what those low, coarse, grunting noises from the carter mean. Puffs of smoke from his short pipe float back on the wind. As we start off on our journey, our hopes and expectations are far off in the distance.

I must have fallen asleep, but I don't know if it happened before we crossed Houtang Stream, or just where it happened. I remember waking up once, and through the cobwebs of my mind I thought I saw the boy who watches over the ducks beckon to me. There was also the parting scene between me and Xiaogen as he straddled his ox. And I could see Grandfather again taking me by the hand and saying, "When you get home tell your granddad to come on over during the cool autumn season and visit the countryside . . . you tell him that your old Grandpa's quail and his quail and his best *gaoliang* wine are waiting here for him to enjoy, with me together . . . you tell him that I can't get around so well anymore; otherwise these past couple of years I would have gone. . . ."

The hollow sound of the wheels wakes me up. The first thing I see is the yellow ox plodding along the road. The carter isn't sitting there by the axle where he should be—there he is, behind the cart. Instead of the whip, he's holding a pipe in his hand. He keeps stroking his chin with his other hand; he is staring off into the horizon. Sister Wuyun is stroking the yellow cat's tail in her lap. She has wrapped her blue cotton scarf around her head below her eyebrows, and the creases on her nose are easier to see than usual, because of the dust that lines them.

They don't know that I'm awake.

"By the third year there were no more letters from him. You soldiers. . . ."

"Was your husband a soldier too?" I couldn't hold back. My carter-uncle pulls me backward by my pigtail.

"And no more letters at all after that?" he asks.

"Since you asked me, I'll tell you. It was just after the Mid-Autumn Festival—I forget which year it was. I had just finished eating breakfast and was slopping the pigs in front of the house. 'Soo-ee, soo-ee!' I didn't even hear Second Mistress from the Wang family of South Village as she came running up, shouting, 'Sister Wuyun, Sister Wuyun! My mother says it's probably a letter from Brother Wuyun!' She held a letter right under my nose. 'Here, let me have it. I want to see. . . .' I don't know why, but I felt sick at heart. Was he still alive? He. . . . My tears fell on the red-bordered envelope, but when I tried to wipe it dry with my hand, all I did was smudge the red border onto the white paper. I threw the slop down in the middle of the yard and went into my room to change into some clean clothes. Then I ran as fast as I could to the school in South Village to see the schoolmaster. I was laughing through my tears. 'I've got a letter here from someone far away; would you please read it to me . . . I haven't had a single word from him for a year.' But after he took the letter from me and read it, he said it was for someone else. I left the letter there in the school and ran home. I didn't go back to feed the pigs or put the chickens to roost; I just went inside and lay down on the *kang*. For days I was like someone whose ghost had left her."

"And no more letters from him at all?"

"None." After unscrewing the lid from the bottle of plum nectar, she drinks a cupful, then another.

"You soldiers, you go away for two or three years, you

say, but do you return home? . . . How many of you ever do? You send your ghosts home for us to see. . . ."

"You mean? . . ." the carter blurts out. "Then he was killed in battle somewhere?"

"That's what it amounted to; not a word for more than a year."

"Well, was he killed in battle or wasn't he?" Jumping down from the cart, he grabs his whip and snaps it in the air a couple of times, making sounds like little explosions.

"What difference does it make? The bitter life of a soldier doesn't allow for much good fortune." Her wrinkled lips look like pieces of torn silk, a sure sign of a fickle nature and a life of misfortune.

As we pass Huang Village the sun begins to set and magpies are flying over the green wheat fields.

"Did you cry when you learned that Brother Wuyun had died in battle?" As I look at her, I continue stroking the yellow cat's tail. But she ignores me and busies herself with straightening her scarf.

The carter scrambles up into the cart by holding on to the handrail and jumping in, landing right above the axle. He is about to smoke; his thick lips are sealed as tightly as the mouth of the bottle.

The flow of words from Sister Wuyun's mouth is like the gentle patter of rain; I stretch out alongside the handrail and before long I've dozed off again.

I awake to discover that the cart is stopped alongside a small village well—the ox is drinking from the well. Sister Wuyun must have been crying, because her sunken eyes are all puffed up and the crows-feet at the sides of her eyes are spread open. Scooping up a bucketful of water from the well, the carter carries it over to the cart.

"Have some—it's nice and cool."

"No, thanks," she replies.

"Go ahead and drink some. If you're not thirsty, at least use some of it to wash your face." He takes a small towel from his waistband and soaks it in the water. "Here, wipe your face. The dust has clouded your eyes."

I can't believe it, a soldier actually offering his towel to someone! That strikes me as peculiar, since the soldiers I've known only know how to fight battles, beat women, and pinch children's ears.

"That winter I traveled to the year-end market where I sold pig bristles. I stood there shouting, 'Good stiff pig bristles . . . fine long pig bristles. . . .' By next year I had just about forgotten my husband . . . didn't think about him at all. But all that did was make me mad at myself, because he might still have been alive. The following autumn I went into the fields with the others to harvest sorghum . . . here, look at my hands—they've seen their share of work. . . .

"I got a more permanent job in the fields the next spring, so I took the baby with me, and the whole family was split up for two or three months. But we got back together the next winter. All kinds of ox hairs . . . pig bristles . . . even some bird feathers, we gathered them up . . . during the winter we gathered them all up, cleaned them, and took them into town to sell when the weather turned warm. If I could catch a ride on a cart, I took Little Baldy into town with me.

"But this time I went in alone. The weather that day

was awful—it had been snowing almost every day—and the year-end market wasn't very crowded. I wouldn't have been able to sell all my pig bristles even if I'd only brought a few bundles. I squatted there in the marketplace from early morning till the sun was setting in the west. Someone had put a poster up on the wall of a large store at the intersection, which everyone stopped to read. I heard that the 'proclamation' had been put up early in the morning . . . or maybe it had only been there since around noontime . . . some of the people read several sentences aloud as they looked at it. I didn't know what it was all about . . . they were saying, 'proclamation this' and 'proclamation that,' but I couldn't figure out just what was being 'proclaimed.' I only knew that a proclamation was the business of officials and had nothing to do with us common folk, so I couldn't figure out why there were so many people interested in it. Someone said it was a proclamation about the capture of some army deserters. I overheard a few other tidbits here and there . . . in a few days the deserters were going to be delivered to the county seat to be shot."

"What year was that? Was that the execution of twenty-odd deserters in 1921?" Absent-mindedly letting down his rolled-up sleeves, the carter rubs his cheekbone with his hand.

"How should. I know what year it was . . . besides, execution or not, what business was it of mine? Anyway, my pig bristles weren't selling so good and things were looking bleak." Rubbing her hands together briefly, she suddenly stretches out her hand as though she were catching a mosquito.

"Someone was reading out the names of the deserters. I looked over at a man in a black gown and said to him, 'Read those names again for me!' At first I was holding the pig bristles in my hand, then I heard him say Jiang Wuyun . . . Jiang Wuyun . . . the name seemed to be echoing in my ears. After a moment or two, I felt like throwing up, like some foul-smelling thing was stuck in my throat; I wanted to swallow it . . . but couldn't . . . my eyes were burning . . . the people looking at the 'proclamation' crowded up in front of it, so I backed off to the side. I tried to move up again and take a look, but my legs wouldn't hold me. More and more people came to look at the 'proclamation,' and I kept backing up . . . farther . . . farther. . . ."

I can see that her forehead and the tip of her nose are beaded with perspiration.

"When I returned to the village it was already late at night. Only when I was getting down from the cart did I remember the pig bristles . . . They'd been the farthest thing from my mind at the time . . . my ears were like two chips of wood . . . my scarf had fallen off, maybe on the road, maybe in the city. . . ."

Now that she has removed her scarf, we can see that her earlobes are missing.

"Just look at these; that's what it means to be a soldier's wife. . . ."

The ends of her scarf, which she has fixed tightly over her head again, move slightly when she speaks.

"Wuyun was still alive, and I felt like going to see him; at least we could be together as husband and wife one last time. . . .

"In February I strapped Little Baldy onto my back and

went into town every day. . . . I heard that the 'proclamation' had been put up several more times, though I never went to see that God-awful thing again. I went to the *yamen* to ask around, but they only said, 'That's none of our business!' They sent me to the military garrison . . . ever since I was a kid I've had a fear of officials . . . a country girl like me. I'd never been to see one of 'em. Those sentries with their bayoneted rifles sent shivers up and down my spine. *Oh, go ahead! After all, they don't just kill people on sight.* Later on, after I'd gone to see them lots of times, I wasn't afraid any longer. After all, out of the three people in our family, they already had one of us in their clutches. They told me that the deserters hadn't been sent over yet. When I asked them when they would be, they told me, 'Wait another month or so.' But when I got back to the village I heard that the deserters had already come from some county seat or other—even today I can't remember which county seat it was, since the only thing that mattered to me was that they had been sent over—and they said if I didn't hurry and go see him, it'd be too late. So I strapped Little Baldy onto my back and went back to town, where I asked around again at the military garrison. 'Why all the impatience?' they asked me. 'How many more hundreds of times are you going to ask? Who knows, maybe they won't be sent over at all.' One day I spotted some big official riding in a horsedrawn carriage with its bells jingling as it came out from the garrison buildings. I put Little Baldy down on the ground and ran over; luckily the carriage was heading toward me, so I knelt down in front of it. . . . I didn't even care if the horse trampled me.

" 'Venerable sir, my husband . . . Jiang Wu—' Before I even got his name out I felt a heavy blow on my shoulders . . . the carriage driver had pushed me over backward. I must've been knocked over. . . . I crawled over to the side of the road. All I could see was that the driver was wearing a military cap.

"I stood up and strapped Little Baldy onto my back again. There was a river in front of the garrison, and for the rest of the afternoon I just sat there on the riverbank looking at the water. Some people were fishing out on the river and some women were washing clothes on the bank. Farther off, at the bend in the river, the water was much deeper, and the crests of waves passed in front of me, one after the other. I don't know how many hundreds of waves I saw passing by as I sat there. I felt like putting Little Baldy down on the riverbank and jumping straight to the bottom. Just leave that one little life behind; as soon as he started crying, someone would surely come and take him away.

"I rubbed his little chest and said something like, 'Little Baldy, you go to sleep.' Then I stroked his little round ears . . . those ears of his, honestly, they're so long and full, just like his daddy's. Looking at his ears, I was seeing his daddy."

A smile of motherly approval spreads across her face.

"I kept on rubbing his chest and said again, 'You go to sleep, Little Baldy.' Then I remembered that I still had a few strings of cash on me, so I decided to put them on his chest. As I reached over . . . reached over to put . . . when I was putting them on his . . . he opened his eyes . . . another sailing boat came around the riverbend, and when I heard the shouts of 'Mama' from a child on the boat, I quickly picked Little Baldy up from the sandbank and held him . . . against my chest. . . ."

Her tears flow along with the motion of her hands as she tightens the scarf under her chin.

"But then . . . then, I knew I had to carry him back home. Even if I had to go begging, at least he would have his mother . . . he deserved a mother."

The corners of her blue scarf quiver with the movements of her cheekbones.

Our path is being crossed by a flock of sheep, herded by a shepherd boy playing a willow flute. The grass and the flowers in the wildwood all blend together, bathed in the slanting rays of the sun, so that all we can see is a vast jumbled patch of yellow.

The carter is now walking alongside the cart, raising trails of dust on the road with the tip of his whip.

" . . . it wasn't until May that the people at the garrison finally told me, 'They'll be coming soon.'

"Toward the end of the month a big steamship pulled up to the wharf in front of the garrison. God, there were a lot of people! Not that many people coming out to watch the river lanterns on the July Fifteenth Festival."

Her sleeves are waving in the air.

"The families of the deserters were standing over to the right, so I moved over there with them. A man in a military cap came over and pinned a kind of badge on each of us. . . . I don't know what they said, since I can't read.

"When they were about to lower the gangplank, a troop of soldiers came up to those of us who were wearing the badges and grouped us into a circle. 'Move a little

farther back from the riverbank; move a little farther. . . .'
They pushed us back some thirty or forty feet away from
the steamship with their rifle butts. An old man with a
white beard stood next to me, holding some packages in
his hand. 'Uncle, why did you bring those things along?' I
asked him. 'Huh? Oh, I have a son and a nephew . . . one
package for each . . . when they get to the next world it
wouldn't be right for them not to have clothes to wear.'

"They lowered the gangplank . . . some of the people
began to cry as soon as they saw the gangplank being lowered . . . me, I wasn't crying. I planted my feet squarely on
the ground and kept my eyes on the ship . . . but no one
came out. After a while, an officer wearing a foreign sword
leaned over the railing and said, 'Have the families move
farther back; they're going to be leaving the ship now.' As
soon as they heard him bark out the order, the soldiers
herded us even farther back with their rifle butts, all the
way back to the bean field by the edge of the road, until
we were standing there on top of the bean shoots. The
gangplank came crashing down, and out they came, led by
an officer, their leg-irons clanking along. I can still see it:
the first one out was a short little man . . . then five or six
more . . . not one of them with broad shoulders like Little
Baldy's daddy . . . really, they looked wretched, their arms
hanging stiffly in front of them. I watched for a long time
before I realized that they were all wearing manacles. The
harder the people around me cried, the calmer I became.
I just kept my eyes on the gangplank. . . . I wanted to ask
Little Baldy's daddy, 'Why couldn't you just be a good
soldier? Why did you have to desert? Look here at your
son; how can you face him?'

"About twenty of them came down, but I couldn't spot

the man I was looking for; from where I stood they all looked the same. A young wife in a green dress lost control and busted through the rifles holding us back . . . they weren't satisfied with just calling her back; no, they went out and grabbed her, and she started rolling in the dirt and crying out, 'He hadn't even been a soldier for three months . . . not even. . . .' Two of them carried her back. Her hair was all mussed up and hanging down in her face. After about the time it takes to smoke a pipeful, they led those of us wearing badges over . . . the more we walked, the closer we got, and the closer we got, the harder it was for me to spot Little Baldy's daddy . . . my eyes started to blur . . . the weeping sounds around me scared me. . . .

"Some of them had cigarettes in their mouths, some were cursing . . . some were even laughing. So this was the stuff soldiers are made of. I guess you could say that soldiers don't give a damn what happens to them.

"I looked them over; Little Baldy's daddy wasn't there for sure. That's strange! I grabbed hold of an officer's belt: 'What about Jiang Wuyun?' 'What's he to you?' 'He's my husband.' I put Little Baldy down on the ground and he started to cry. I slapped him in the mouth, then I began hitting the officer. 'What have you done with him?'

"'Good for you, lady, we're with you. . . .' The prisoners were shouting from where they were crouching. When the officer saw what was happening, he quickly called some soldiers over to drag me away. 'It's not only Jiang Wuyun,' he said. 'There are a couple of others who haven't been sent over yet; they'll be over in a day or two on the next ship. Those three were the ringleaders of this group of deserters.'

"I put the child on my back and left the riverbank, with

the badge still pinned on, and walked off. My legs were all rubbery. The streets were filled with people who had come over to watch the excitement. I was walking behind the garrison buildings, and there at the base of the garrison wall sat the old man with the two packages, but now he only had one left. 'Uncle, didn't your son come either?' I asked him. He just arched his back and stuck the ends of his beard into his mouth and chewed on them as he wept.

"He told me, 'Since he was one of the ringleaders, they carried out their capital punishment on the spot.' At the time I didn't know what capital punishment meant. . . ."

At this point she begins to ramble.

"Three years later, when Little Baldy was eight, I sent him to the beancurd shop . . . that's what I did. I go to see him twice a year and he comes home once every two years, but then only for ten days or a couple of weeks. . . ."

The carter has left the side of the cart and is walking along a little path, his hands clasped behind his back. With the sun off to the side, he casts a long shadow which divides with every step he takes.

"I have a family too. . . ." The words seem to fall from his lips, as though he is speaking to the wildwood.

"Huh?" As Sister Wuyun loosens her scarf a little, the wrinkles above her nose quiver momentarily, "Really? You're out of the army, and still you don't go home?"

"What's that? Go home, you say! You mean go home with nothing but the clothes on my back?" The carter sneers as he rubs his nose hard with his coarse hand.

"Haven't you put a little something away these past few years?"

"That's exactly why I deserted, to make a little money if I could." He cinches his belt tighter.

I put on another cotton jacket and Sister Wuyun throws a blanket over her shoulders. "Um! Still another mile to go; Now if we had a harness horse . . . um! We could be there in nothing flat! An ox is no good. This beast just plods along with no spirit, and it's no good at all on a battlefield."

The carter open his straw bag and takes out a padded jacket from which pieces of straw fall off and swirl in the wind. He puts it on.

The winds at dusk are just like February winds. In the rear of the cart the carter opens up the wine jug that my mother's father had given my father's father.

"Here, drink! As they say, 'In the midst of a journey open a jug of wine, for the poor love to gamble.' Now for two cups of wine." After drinking several cups, he opens his shirt and exposes his chest. He is chewing on some pieces of jerky, causing frothy bubbles to gather at the corners of his mouth. Whenever a gust of wind blows across his face, the bubbles on his lips expand a little.

As we near the town, through the gray overcast we can tell only that it is not a patch of open country, nor a mountain range, nor the seashore, nor a forest. . . . The closer our cart comes to the town, the more it seems to recede into the distance. The pores on our faces and hands feel sticky. Another look ahead, and this time even the end of the road is lost from view. The carter puts the wine jug away and picks up his whip. By now the ox's horns have grown indistinct.

"Haven't you returned home or even received a letter

since you left?" The carter hasn't heard her. He blows on his whistle to urge the ox on. Then he jumps down from the cart and walks along up front with the animal. An empty cart with a red lantern hanging from its axle comes rolling up to us.

"A heavy fog!"

"It sure is!"

The carters are calling out to each other.

"A heavy fog in March . . . that either means war or a year of drought. . . ."

The two carts pass on the road.

Translated by Howard Goldblatt

KIRK A. DENTON teaches at The Ohio State University, where he offers courses in Chinese literature, film, and popular culture. He is editor of the journal *Modern Chinese Literature and Culture*, manager of the online MCLC Resource Center, and moderator of the MCLC LIST, a listserv devoted to scholarly discussion on the culture of modern and contemporary China. His edited collection, *Modern Chinese Literary Thought: Writings on Literature, 1893–1945*, was published by Stanford University Press in 1996. Two years later, his *The Problematic of Self in Modern Chinese Literature: Hu Feng and Lu Ling* was also published by Stanford. He is associate editor of the Chinese section of *The Columbia Companion to Modern East Asian Literature* (Columbia, 2003) and a coeditor of *China: Adapting the Past, Confronting the Future* (Center for Chinese Studies, University of Michigan, 2002). He is coeditor of *Literary Societies in Republican China* (Lexington, 2008). He has published several articles on museum culture, and he is currently writing a book on the politics of historical representation in museums and memorial sites in Greater China, entitled *Exhibiting the Past: The Politics and Ideology of Museums in the People's Republic of China, Taiwan, and Hong Kong*.